DISNEYLAND PARIS

TRAVEL GUIDE 2024

The Up-to-Date Tips for Exploring the Rides, Shows and Other Unmissable Attractions in the Heart of France.

By

Anita Whitacre

Copyright©2024 ANITA WHITACRE

All rights reserved. Without the prior written permission of the publisher, no portion of this publication may be reproduced, stored in a retrieval system, or transmitted in any form or by any means, electronic, mechanical, photocopying, recording, or otherwise.

CONTENTS

INTRODUCTION 5

    Brief History And Unique Features 8

    Cultural Aspects Setting It Apart From Other Disney Parks 10

IMPORTANT THINGS TO KNOW BEFORE YOU GO 13

    Why Visit Disneyland Paris? 13

    Choosing The Right Time To Visit 15

    Creating An Itinerary 18

        1-Day Itinerary for Adults 18

        2-Days Detailed Itinery for Couples 21

        3-Days Detailed Itinery for Families 28

    Packing List (Essentials) 34

    Park Rules & Regulations 37

    Accessibility Information For Special Guests 39

PLANNING YOUR VISIT 45

    Opening Hours 45

    Location Of Disneyland Paris 47

    Getting Your Tickets Ready 48

Overview Of Accommodation Options 54

Booking Tips And Considerations 62

GETTING TO DISNEYLAND PARIS 65

Transportation Options 65

Overview Of On-Site Facilities 68

THEME PARKS 71

Disneyland Park & Walt Disney Studios 72

Detailed Guide To Rides And Attractions In Each Park 77

Must-See Highlights And Hidden Gems 91

Exploring Disney Village 94

GUIDE TO SHOWS, PARADES AND EVENTS 99

Thrilling Shows 99

Captivating Parades 102

Seasonal Celebrations 106

SKIP THE LINE, NIGHT TOURS, AND ENTRANCES 115

Strategies For Reducing Wait Times 117

Information On Nighttime Experiences 120

Guidance On Park Entrances 121

RESTAURANTS AND FAMILY TRAVEL 125

Dining Options Within The Parks And Resort Hotels 125

Recommendations For Family-Friendly Dining 141

The Right Place To Go Shopping 144

Tips For Traveling With Children 152

VISITOR TIPS **155**

Insider Tips And Tricks For A Successful Visit 155

Suggestions For Managing Crowds 157

Interesting Facts About Disneyland Paris 159

CONCLUSION **163**

Recap Of Key Points 163

Final Thouths 166

INTRODUCTION

Welcome, fellow adventurers, and seekers of magic! If you hold this book in your hands, you're on the brink of embarking on a journey beyond your wildest imaginations—a journey to the enchanting realm of Disneyland Paris. As your guide, let me introduce myself. I'm Anita Whitacre, a storyteller, traveler, and lifelong lover of all things magical. And today, I'm thrilled to invite you into a world where dreams come true and fantasies become reality.

Picture this: a fresh morning in spring, the smell of freshly baked pastries drifting through the air, and the excitement buzzing in your veins as you step through the gates of Disneyland Paris. The magic here is tangible—it wraps around you like a warm hug, whispering promises of adventure and wonder. But before we dive headfirst into the thrills and delights that await, allow me to share a personal tale—a story that sparked my passion for exploration and set me on the path to becoming your trusted guide.

It was a sunny afternoon many years ago when my parents surprised me with a trip to Disneyland Paris. I still remember the feeling of pure disbelief and joy as we drove through the gates, greeted by the iconic Sleeping Beauty Castle standing tall against the blue sky. As a wide-eyed child, every part of the park held the promise of a new adventure, from flying with Peter Pan to soaring through the stars with Buzz Lightyear.

But amidst the laughter and excitement, it was the little moments that made the biggest impression—the shared smiles, the whispered secrets, the feeling of being truly alive in a world where anything was possible. That trip ignited a spark within me—a desire for exploration, a love for storytelling, and a deep appreciation for the magic that exists in everyday life.

Since that memorable day, I've returned to Disneyland Paris time and time again, each visit revealing new wonders and reigniting that sense of childlike wonder. And now, dear reader, it's my honor and privilege to pass on that magic to you. Within the pages of this guide, you'll find everything you need to create your own unforgettable Disneyland Paris adventure—a roadmap to the happiest place on earth, tailored to your every desire.

But before we delve into the details, let me assure you of one thing: this is more than just a travel guide. It's a companion, a confidant, and a fellow dreamer on your journey through the enchanted realms of Disneyland Paris. So, whether you're a first-time visitor or a seasoned explorer, buckle up and get ready to be whisked away on the adventure of a lifetime. Together, we'll uncover the secrets of Disneyland Paris, one magical moment at a time.

In the chapters that follow, we'll explore every corner of this wonderful kingdom, from the famous attractions to the hidden gems known only to the most daring travelers. We'll taste delicious treats, meet beloved characters, and revel in the joy of simply being alive in a place where dreams take flight. But above all, we'll create memories that will last a lifetime— memories of laughter, love, and the pure joy of living life to the fullest.

So, dear reader, are you ready to embark on the adventure of a lifetime? Are you prepared to let go of your inhibitions, embrace your inner child, and immerse yourself in the magic of Disneyland Paris? If so, then join me as we journey into a world where dreams come true and every day is a new adventure. Welcome to Disneyland Paris—where the magic never ends, and the possibilities are limitless.

Brief History And Unique Features of Disneyland Paris

Alright, let's delve into the captivating world of Disneyland Paris and explore its intriguing history and unique features. As we embark on this journey together, I'll guide you through the magical development of this famous destination.

Imagine entering a place where fairy tales come true and dreams soar. That's Disneyland Paris, where magic has no limits. As I narrate its beginnings, you'll uncover the vision and creativity that brought this enchanting place to life.

It all began in the early 1990s when the Walt Disney Company aimed to bring the beloved magic of Disneyland to Europe. After careful planning, Disneyland Paris welcomed visitors on April 12, 1992. Located near Paris in Marne-la-Vallée, this expansive resort quickly won the hearts of guests from near and far.

However, Disneyland Paris isn't just a copy of its American counterparts; it has its own special charm. Once you step inside, you're transported to a world where fantasy and reality blend seamlessly. The park's design reflects the diverse cultures of

Europe, featuring enchanting lands inspired by fairy tales, folklore, and famous landmarks.

One of Disneyland Paris's standout features is its breathtaking architecture and meticulous attention to detail. Every corner is adorned with intricate designs and whimsical touches that inspire wonder. Whether you're strolling down Main Street, U.S.A., or exploring the medieval streets of Fantasyland, you'll be surrounded by a colorful array of themes and textures.

What truly distinguishes Disneyland Paris is its dedication to storytelling and immersion. Each attraction isn't just a ride; it's an immersive experience that transports you to another world. Whether it's thrilling adventures or heartwarming encounters with beloved characters, every moment is filled with Disney's magic.

Another highlight of Disneyland Paris is its focus on live entertainment and spectacle. From dazzling parades to breathtaking fireworks displays, the park offers a feast for the senses. Whether you're watching Mickey and friends dance down Main Street or enjoying the nighttime show at Sleeping Beauty Castle, you're sure to be captivated by unforgettable moments.

Yet, the most magical aspect of Disneyland Paris is the memories it creates for visitors of all ages. Whether it's your first visit or a return to cherished moments, the park holds a special place in the hearts of millions worldwide. It's a place where laughter fills the air, dreams come true, and Disney's magic unites people in extraordinary ways.

So, as you prepare for your adventure to Disneyland Paris, remember you're not just visiting a theme park; you're entering a realm of endless possibilities and timeless enchantment. With each step, may your heart be filled with the wonder and joy that only Disneyland Paris can offer.

Cultural Aspects Setting It Apart From Other Disney Parks

Let's explore the special cultural aspects and themes that make Disneyland Paris different from other Disney parks. As someone who has visited this magical place firsthand, I can assure you that Disneyland Paris offers a captivating mix of European charm and classic Disney magic.

When you enter Disneyland Paris, you're not just going to a theme park; you're starting a trip through the rich tapestry of European culture and history. From the moment you arrive, you'll notice the unique architectural styles and themes that honor the diverse cultures of Europe.

One of the cultural highlights of Disneyland Paris is its celebration of French art, literature, and food. From the famous Sleeping Beauty Castle inspired by the castles of the Loire Valley to the fun Ratatouille: The Adventure ride set in the busy streets of Paris, the park combines French culture and Disney stories in a delightful way.

But Disneyland Paris isn't just about France; it also honors the variety of European heritage. In Adventureland, you can go on an exciting journey through exotic jungles and ancient ruins inspired by Europe's colonial era of exploration. Meanwhile, Frontierland takes you to the wild landscapes of the American West, where you can experience the Gold Rush excitement and meet iconic frontier characters.

One of the most loved parts of Disneyland Paris is its seasonal festivals and events, which celebrate European traditions throughout the year. From the bright colors of the Spring Festival to the spooky fun of Halloween, each season offers new experiences that reflect the cultural richness of the continent.

Besides its themed areas, Disneyland Paris welcomes visitors from all backgrounds, with attractions and entertainment for everyone. Whether you're a thrill-seeker wanting to try the Tower of Terror or a young fan meeting your favorite Disney princess, there's something for all ages at the park.

Disneyland Paris is exceptional not only for its top-notch attractions and entertainment but also for its celebration of European culture and history. From its famous landmarks to its themed areas, the park offers an enchanting experience that captures the essence of the continent in a Disney way. So, if you're ready for a magical journey through Europe, Disneyland Paris is waiting for you.

IMPORTANT THINGS TO KNOW BEFORE YOU GO

Before you pack your bags and head off to the enchanting world of Disneyland Paris, there are a few important things you should know. Believe me, I've been there, and I want to ensure your trip is as easy and fun as can be. So, let's begin by discussing some crucial advice and techniques to assist you in getting the most out of your Disneyland Paris experience. From the optimal times to visit to what essentials to bring, I've got you covered. So, sit back, relax, and let's delve into the essential details before you set off on your Disney adventure!

Why Visit Disneyland Paris?

I'll be sharing with you why a trip to Disneyland Paris should be at the top of your travel bucket list.

1. First and foremost, let's talk about its uniqueness. Did you know that outside the United States, there are only

four Disneyland parks worldwide? And guess what? Disneyland Paris proudly stands as the only one in Europe. Yes, you heard it right! Nestled in the heart of France, Disneyland Paris invites travelers from all around the world to experience its exceptional charm and appeal.

2. Now, let's explore the nostalgic atmosphere that fills every corner of this magical place. From the moment you step into Disneyland Paris, you'll be transported back to your happiest childhood memories. Imagine walking down Main Street, U.S.A., hand in hand with beloved Disney characters you've come to adore over the years. From the famous Mickey Mouse to the enchanting Disney Princesses and even the powerful Avengers, Disneyland Paris is a sanctuary where dreams become real and memories are cherished forever.

3. But wait, there's more! Disneyland Paris isn't just a theme park; it's the ultimate family vacation spot. Situated close to the lively city of Paris, Disneyland Paris offers the perfect getaway for families seeking fun and adventure. Whether you're enjoying an exciting roller coaster ride, watching a dazzling parade, or immersing yourself in the magic of a live show, there's something here for every family member to delight in.

4. And let's not forget about the convenience. With its strategic location outside Paris, Disneyland Paris is an ideal day trip for families wanting to maximize their time in the city of lights. Picture starting your day with a leisurely breakfast in Paris, then taking a train to Disneyland Paris to spend the day exploring the enchanting attractions of the park. It's the perfect recipe for an unforgettable family escapade!

Choosing The Right Time To Visit

When planning your trip to Disneyland Paris, timing is crucial to ensure the best experience possible. As your trusted travel guide, I'll walk you through the best times to visit, considering weather conditions, crowd levels, and special events that add extra magic to your adventure.

Peak and Low Seasons

Let's begin by discussing peak and low seasons at Disneyland Paris. Peak season usually spans from June to August, coinciding with the summer months when families visit the parks for vacation. During this time, you can expect warmer temperatures and longer daylight hours, perfect for maximizing your time on rides and exploring the parks. However, with more people attending, there are larger crowds and longer wait times for attractions.

On the other hand, the low season at Disneyland Paris falls between January and March. During these months, crowds tend to lessen, providing a more relaxed atmosphere for visitors to enjoy. Additionally, you may find lower prices on accommodations and special promotions during this time, making it an ideal option for budget-conscious travelers. Keep in mind that the weather during the low season can be cooler, so be sure to pack accordingly.

Weekdays or Weekends

Another aspect to consider when planning your visit is whether to go on weekdays or weekends. Weekdays generally have fewer crowds compared to weekends, especially during peak season. If possible, aim to visit the parks on a weekday to take advantage of shorter lines and a more relaxed pace. However, if your schedule only allows for a weekend visit, don't worry! With proper planning and strategic timing, you can still make the most of your experience, even during busier times.

During Festivals

Disneyland Paris hosts several special events and festivals throughout the year, adding an extra layer of excitement to your visit. From seasonal celebrations like Halloween and Christmas to themed festivals like the Marvel Season of Super Heroes, there's always something special happening at the parks.

Attending these festivals can enhance your Disneyland Paris experience, offering unique entertainment, themed decorations, and exclusive merchandise. However, it's important to note that certain festivals may attract larger crowds, particularly during peak season. To make the most of these events, consider visiting during off-peak times or using early morning and evening hours when crowds tend to be lighter.

Weather

Now, let's talk about the weather. Being prepared for the elements can make or break your Disney adventure. Summer months, from June to August, bring warm temperatures and longer daylight hours, perfect for enjoying outdoor attractions and nighttime shows. However, be prepared for occasional rain showers and higher humidity levels. On the flip side, winter months, especially December and January, can be chilly with shorter daylight hours. But there's something truly magical about experiencing Disneyland Paris adorned in twinkling lights and festive decorations during the holiday season. Spring and autumn offer milder temperatures and fewer crowds, making them ideal times to visit if you're looking for pleasant weather and shorter queues.

The best time to visit Disneyland Paris depends on your preferences and priorities. Whether you're looking to avoid crowds, enjoy seasonal events, or soak up the sunshine, there's a perfect time for everyone. Just remember to plan ahead, pack accordingly, and embrace the magic of Disney, no matter when you decide to go.

Creating An Itinerary

1-Day Itinerary for Adults

Are you dreaming of a wonderful day at Disneyland Paris? Well, get ready because I'm about to take you on an adventure-filled journey through the most magical place on earth! Let's explore your ideal 1-day plan for grown-ups, designed to make the most of every moment at this amazing destination.

Morning at Disneyland Paris (8:30/9:30 am to noon)

As the sun rises over the famous Sleeping Beauty Castle, it's time to start your day of fun and thrills. First off, grab a satisfying breakfast at one of the cozy cafes or bakeries on Main Street, U.S.A. Trust me; you'll need lots of energy for the exciting day ahead.

After breakfast, let's head straight to the heart of the magic – Disneyland Park! Begin your morning by enjoying some of the classic rides like Space Mountain: Mission 2 or Indiana Jones and the Temple of Peril. Feel the excitement as you zoom through space or brave the adventurous jungle – the choice is yours!

Next, dive into the charming world of Fantasyland. Take a walk through the delightful gardens of Alice's Curious Labyrinth or go on a nostalgic trip aboard Peter Pan's Flight. And don't forget to take a photo with your favorite Disney characters along the way – because memories make the best souvenirs!

Afternoon at Disneyland Paris (12 pm – 4 pm)

After an exciting morning, it's time to refuel and recharge. Head to one of the park's many restaurants for a tasty lunch break. Whether you fancy a fancy meal at Walt's – An American Restaurant or a quick snack at Casey's Corner, Disneyland Paris offers something for every taste.

With your energy replenished, it's time to explore more of the park's attractions.

Dive into the underwater world of Discoveryland and discover the amazing wonders of the Nautilus. Then, venture into Adventureland for an adventurous journey on Pirates of the Caribbean.

As the afternoon sun casts a golden glow over the park, take a leisurely stroll along the scenic paths of Frontierland. Admire the breathtaking views of Big Thunder Mountain or enjoy a peaceful cruise along the Rivers of the Far West. With so much to see and do, your afternoon is sure to be full of excitement and fun!

Evening at Disneyland Paris (4 pm to closing time)

As the day winds down, it's time to create some magical memories that will last a lifetime. Begin your evening with a trip to Walt Disney Studios Park, where you can immerse yourself in the glamour of Hollywood. Watch an exciting stunt show at Moteurs... Action! or go on a backstage tour of the Studio Tram Tour: Behind the Magic.

As night falls, Disneyland Paris turns into a dazzling show of lights and music. Don't miss the spectacular Disney Illuminations show, where iconic Disney moments come to life in an enchanting display of fireworks and special effects. Afterward, take a leisurely walk through the beautifully lit park, savoring every moment of your enchanted evening.

As closing time approaches, take one last look around and soak in the magic of Disneyland Paris. Reflect on the amazing experiences you've had throughout the day and treasure the memories you've created.

2-Days Detailed Itinery for Couples

> Day 1: A Magical Adventure at Disneyland Park

Morning:

Begin your day with an exciting ride on Space Mountain roller coaster. This thrilling experience is suitable for everyone, from young teens to adults, and is located in the Discoveryland section of Disneyland Park. Get ready for an out-of-this-world journey like no other!

Then, join the mission to defeat Emperor Zurg in Buzz Lightyear's laser game. This interactive activity is great for guests of all ages, including children, teenagers, adults, and even toddlers. Team up with Buzz Lightyear and put your skills to the test in this fun challenge situated in Discoveryland.

After your thrilling adventures, take a relaxed walk through Alice's Labyrinth. This charming maze is a delightful treat for visitors of all ages and little ones. It's situated in the Fantasyland area of Disneyland Park, offering an enchanting experience inspired by Lewis Carroll's timeless story.

No trip to Disneyland Paris would be complete without a visit to Sleeping Beauty's castle. This iconic landmark is a must-see for everyone, including toddlers, and is located at the heart of Fantasyland. Be amazed by the beauty of this fairy tale castle and capture wonderful memories with your family.

Take flight with Peter Pan and journey to Neverland. This enchanting ride is suitable for guests of all ages, including young children, and is located in Fantasyland. Join Peter Pan, Wendy, and the Lost Boys on a magical adventure through the night sky.

Then, dive into the thrilling adventure of Pirates of the Caribbean. This timeless attraction is perfect for guests of all ages, including young children, and is situated in the Adventureland section of Disneyland Park. Join Captain Jack Sparrow and experience the excitement of high-seas escapades.

Afternoon:

Recharge your energy at the beautiful Blue Lagoon Restaurant. Tucked in Adventureland inside Disneyland Park, this tropical paradise offers a lovely dining experience among the lush surroundings of the Pirates of the Caribbean attraction.

After filling up, it's time to visit Robinson's Cabin. Suitable for everyone, especially young kids, this hidden treasure is nestled in the heart of Adventureland. Take a walk through this delightful wilderness getaway and immerse yourself in the adventurous spirit inspired by the classic story of Robinson Crusoe.

Next, gear up for an exciting adventure on the famous Indiana Jones roller coaster. Situated in Adventureland, this thrilling ride is a must for tweens, teens, and adults alike. Get ready for twists, turns, and surprises as you venture into the depths of the Temple of Doom.

But the fun doesn't stop there! Jump on the railroad for an exciting journey on Big Thunder Mountain. Suitable for all ages, including kids, tweens, teens, and adults, this exhilarating trip through the Wild West promises excitement at every corner. Hold on tight as you zoom through rugged canyons and mysterious caves on this runaway mine train adventure.

Evening:

As the day winds down, venture into the spooky halls of Phantom Manor. Located in Frontierland, this chilling attraction is great for everyone, from kids to adults and even brave toddlers! Get ready to be scared as you explore the ghostly corridors of this haunted house and uncover its secrets.

And what better way to end your day of adventure than with a captivating night show? Join Mickey and friends for a fantastic display of lights, music, and magic that will leave you in awe. It's the perfect way to wrap up your unforgettable day at Disneyland Paris.

> Day 2: Walt Disney Studios

Feel Like a Hollywood Star:

Start your day feeling like a movie star as you step into Studio 1, located right at the entrance of Walt Disney Studios in the Front Lot. Take in the grandeur of this Hollywood-themed setting, where every corner exudes glamour and charm.

Frozen Animation Celebration:

Make sure to arrive early for the Frozen Animation Celebration, an enchanting show located in the heart of Walt Disney Studios' Front Lot. Join Anna, Elsa, and Olaf as they captivate audiences with their magical performances and heartwarming story.

Trip to Route 66:

Experience the excitement of a lifetime as you journey down Route 66 on the Cars Road Trip attraction, located in the Worlds of Pixar section of Walt Disney Studios. Feel the wind in your hair as you race alongside Lightning McQueen and Mater in this fast-paced adventure.

Experience the Feel of a Parachute Drop:

Prepare to have your heart racing as you experience the adrenaline rush of a parachute drop in the Worlds of Pixar area of Walt Disney Studios. Feel the excitement build as you ascend to new heights before freefalling back to earth in this thrilling ride.

Step into Toy Story:

Embark on a playful adventure in the world of Toy Story as you hop aboard the Slinky Dog ZigZag Spin attraction, located in the Worlds of Pixar section of Walt Disney Studios. Feel the excitement of the spin as you whirl and twirl through Andy's backyard.

Experience the Adventure of Ratatouille:

Delight your senses in the culinary delights of Ratatouille as you dive into the adventure of this beloved film in Walt Disney Studios' Worlds of Pixar area. Join Remy on a whimsical journey through Gusteau's kitchen in this immersive 4D experience.

Have a Lunch Break:

Refuel and recharge at Bistroz Chez Remy, a charming restaurant inspired by the world of Ratatouille. Located in the Worlds of Pixar section, this culinary gem offers a variety of menus ranging from 30 to 65€, ensuring there's something for every palate.

Alternatively, grab a quick bite at Restaurant en Coulisse, located behind Disney Studio 1, offering a range of breakfast items, salads, and burgers to satisfy your hunger.

Accelerate Without Limits at RC Racer:

Hold on tight as you accelerate without limits on RC Racer, located in the Worlds of Pixar area of Walt Disney Studios. Feel the excitement of the race as you zoom up and down the towering half-pipe track in this exhilarating ride.

An Unforgettable Ride on Crush's Coaster:

Embark on an unforgettable underwater adventure on Crush's Coaster, located in the Worlds of Pixar section of Walt Disney Studios. Join Nemo and friends as you whirl and swirl through the ocean depths in this thrilling roller coaster experience.

Say Goodbye to Walt Disney Studios:

End your day on a high note with a visit to the Tower of Terror, located in the Production Courtyard of Walt Disney Studios. Brace yourself for a hair-raising drop as you plunge into the Twilight Zone in this iconic attraction.

Go Home with a Souvenir:

Before you leave, be sure to stop by one of the many stores scattered throughout Walt Disney Studios to pick up a souvenir or two to commemorate your unforgettable adventure.

With this action-packed itinerary, your day 2 at Walt Disney Studios is sure to be filled with excitement, laughter, and memories that will last a lifetime.

3-Days Detailed Itinery for Families

> ### Day 1: Walt Disney Studios

If you're planning a 3-day adventure with your family at Disneyland Paris, get ready because I've got an exciting plan for you. Let's start with Day 1 together!

Morning:

First things first, check into your comfortable hotel at Disneyland Paris. You've got some great choices like Disney's Hotel Cheyenne, Disney's Hotel Santa Fe, or Disney's Sequoia Lodge. Choose one and settle in for a magical stay.

Now, it's time to begin your day at Walt Disney Studios Park with a thrilling ride on the Twilight Zone Tower of Terror. Brace yourself for an exciting journey as you drop into the depths of this spooky elevator shaft. Watch out for surprises, especially the ghostly little girl!

After that adrenaline rush, head to the Ratatouille: The Adventure ride. This 4D experience will take you on an exciting culinary journey through Gusteau's restaurant kitchen. It's great for all ages, but maybe not suitable for the youngest ones!

Afternoon:

Feeling hungry? Go to the cozy Bistrot Chez Rémy restaurant for a delicious Parisian lunch. Situated near the Ratatouille ride, it's the perfect place to eat and unwind.

Now, get ready for more excitement with Crush's Coaster. Join Nemo and friends on a thrilling adventure through the Great Barrier Reef, with twists, turns, and exhilarating flips.

Next up, it's time to speed around on the RC Racer ride. Feel the thrill as you race around in a toy car on this exciting attraction.

Evening:

Back at the hotel, take a well-deserved rest and recharge for the evening ahead.

As night falls, head to Disneyland Park for the stunning Disney Illuminations show. Enjoy the amazing fireworks, dazzling lights, and enchanting projections on Sleeping Beauty Castle. It's a magical show you won't want to miss!

> ➢ Day 2: Disneyland Park

Alright, let's dive into your magical 3-day adventure at Disneyland Paris, focusing on Day 2.

Morning:

As the sun rises over Disneyland Paris, get ready for an exciting start at Disneyland Park. Feel your heart race on the famous Big Thunder Mountain Railroad, a thrilling roller coaster that takes you through the rocky terrain of the Old West. Feel the breeze in your hair as you twist and turn through rocky caves and deserted mines.

Next, go on a thrilling adventure through the Indiana Jones and the Temple of Peril ride. Prepare for fast twists and turns as you navigate through the dangerous ruins of a cursed temple. Will you come out safely or fall victim to the temple's ancient curse?

Afternoon:

After building up an appetite with all the excitement, head to Adventureland for a delicious meal at Hakuna Matata restaurant. Enjoy tasty kebabs, fresh salads, and flavorful rice dishes inspired by African cuisines. Let the lively atmosphere take you to the heart of the Pride Lands.

While in Adventureland, don't miss the enchanting Festival of the Lion King show. Immerse yourself in the captivating world of Simba and his friends as they entertain you with stunning performances and catchy rhythms. It's a celebration of love, friendship, and the cycle of life that will leave you amazed.

Feeling the urge for some Star Wars action? Go to Discoveryland and join the Rebel Alliance as a pilot for the Star Wars Hyperspace Mountain roller coaster. Travel to a distant galaxy as you embark on a daring mission to spy on the Imperial Star Destroyer. May the Force be with you!

Finish off your afternoon with a relaxing trip on the Pirates of the Caribbean boat ride. Sail through mysterious caves and dangerous waters as you encounter adventurous pirates, stolen treasures, and perhaps even a ghostly curse or two. It's an exciting adventure you'll remember for a long time.

Evening:

As the day comes to an end, head to Disney Village for a taste of the Wild West at Buffalo Bill's Wild West Show. Immerse yourself in a thrilling display of cowboy showdowns, Indian dances, and daring stunts, all against the backdrop of the wild frontier. Enjoy delicious Texan-style food as you cheer on the action-packed show.

> Day 3: Avenger's HQ

Morning:

Let's start our third day at Disneyland Paris with an exciting adventure at the Avengers' Headquarters. Get ready for a thrilling ride on Flight Force, where you'll travel through space at super-fast speeds, dodging missiles and helping Iron Man and Captain Marvel save the universe. And for those who want a different kind of fun, go to the Spider-Man W.E.B. adventure nearby to deal with some annoying Spider-bots.

After that, get ready for the exciting RC Racer ride. Feel the excitement as you race along on a toy car at very fast speeds, enjoying the thrill of the race.

Before we finish our morning adventures, make sure to see the amazing Avengers Unite show. See the Marvel Avengers Campus come alive with epic battles, featuring your favorite heroes like Black Widow and Black Panther fighting against the tough Taskmaster and his group of mercenaries.

Afternoon:

Now that we're hungry, let's go to the Earl of Sandwich restaurant in Disney Village for a tasty lunch. Recharge for the adventures ahead.

Next, dive into the world of Disney animation at the Art of Disney Animation attraction. Learn about the history of Disney's famous characters and stories, and try drawing your favorite Disney friends.

End your afternoon with a fantastic performance of Mickey and the Magician. Let the beautiful music and captivating stories take you to a world of joy and happiness, saying goodbye to Disneyland Paris in true Disney style.

Evening:

As the sun sets, it's time to say goodbye to Disneyland Paris and explore the heart of Paris itself. Go to Port de la Bourdonnais, near the Eiffel Tower, to take a scenic cruise along the Seine River.

As you pass famous landmarks like Notre Dame and the Eiffel Tower, enjoy the stunning views of Parisian beauty all around you. With the help of an informative audioguide, learn about the history and importance of each sight along the way.

Feel free to step onto the open-air decks of the boat, letting the cool evening breeze refresh you as you enjoy the romantic atmosphere of Paris at night.

And remember, if you'd rather save this enchanting cruise for the next day, your flexible ticket lets you board at any time. So, whether you decide to relax that evening or start your magical journey the next morning, the beauty of Paris is ready for you to enjoy at your own pace.

Packing List (Essentials)

When you're getting ready to start your exciting journey to Disneyland Paris, it's really important to pack smartly to make sure you have a smooth and fun experience. Let's talk about some packing basics that will help you enjoy your time in the happiest place on earth.

1. Tickets and Disney Passes

First of all, don't forget your tickets and Disney passes. These are like your special keys to unlock all the wonders of Disneyland Paris. Make sure you double-check to have them safely packed in your bag before leaving home. It would be a real bummer to get to the park and realize you forgot your tickets!

2. A Small Backpack

Next, a small backpack is your best buddy for exploring the parks. Pick a light, comfy backpack that can carry all your important stuff without making you feel heavy. It's perfect for keeping your things safe while you wander around Main Street, U.S.A. or go on cool adventures in Adventureland.

3. Sunscreen

Sunscreen is a must, even if it's cloudy. Protect your skin from the sun's rays by putting on sunscreen before going outside. Remember to reapply during the day, especially if you'll be out in the sun for a while.

4. Comfy Shoes

Comfy shoes are super important for a day at Disneyland Paris. You'll be walking a lot, so choose supportive sneakers or walking shoes that'll keep your feet happy from morning to night.

5. A Reusable Water Bottle

Staying hydrated is really important, especially on hot summer days. Bring a reusable water bottle to sip on throughout the day. There are water fountains all over the parks where you can refill your bottle for free, helping you stay cool and energized.

6. Snacks

Don't forget to bring some snacks to keep hunger away between meals. Granola bars, trail mix, or fruit snacks are easy options that'll give you a quick energy boost without weighing you down.

7. A hat

A hat not only looks cool but also gives you shade on sunny days. Pick a wide-brimmed hat to protect your face and neck from the sun while adding some style to your outfit.

8. A Power Bank

In today's world, a power bank is a lifesaver. Since you'll be taking lots of photos and videos all day, your phone's battery might run out fast. Keep a fully charged power bank in your backpack so you never miss capturing a magical moment.

9. A Pen and Paper

A pen and paper might seem old-fashioned nowadays, but they can be useful for jotting down notes, keeping track of showtimes, or even writing down special memories.

10. An Umbrella

An umbrella is a smart thing to pack, especially if you're visiting during the rainy season. While Disneyland Paris is magical in any weather, staying dry can make your experience even better.

11. Your Wallet And A Way To Pay

Obviously, you'll need your wallet and a way to pay for any souvenirs or snacks you want to buy. Whether you like cash or card, make sure you have enough to cover any costs during your visit.

12. Tissues

Tissues are useful to have on hand for wiping away tears of joy during the fireworks or cleaning up spills.

13. Hand Sanitizer

Lastly, don't forget to bring hand sanitizer. With so many people visiting the parks every day, it's important to keep your hands clean to avoid getting sick. A small bottle of hand sanitizer is easy to carry in your backpack and will give you peace of mind during your visit.

Park Rules & Regulations And Guest Conduct Policies

When it comes to having fun at Disneyland Paris, it's crucial to understand the park rules, regulations, and how guests should behave. These guidelines are meant to keep everyone safe and make sure everyone has a good time. As your travel expert, let me explain these rules clearly and simply.

- Firstly, some things are not allowed in the park. Selfie sticks, drones, and remote-controlled toys are examples. These rules help keep guests safe and maintain the magical feeling of the park.

- Also, certain types of transportation like scooters, skateboards, hoverboards, and similar things are not allowed in Disneyland Paris. However, if someone needs a medically recognized device for mobility assistance, they can bring it.

- Regarding clothing, guests must follow the park's dress code. They should dress appropriately for a family-friendly place and avoid anything too revealing or inappropriate. While costumes are encouraged for younger guests, adults shouldn't wear them unless it's a special event approved by the park.

- Taking photos is popular, but guests should be aware of the rules about using flash and taking commercial photos. Flash isn't allowed in some areas to avoid bothering others or disturbing wildlife. Also, taking professional photos with tripods and lights isn't allowed without permission from the park.

- To ensure everyone's safety and comfort, some things are strictly banned in the park. This includes alcoholic drinks, glass bottles, weapons, or anything that looks like a weapon. Also, noisy things like horns, loudspeakers, and vuvuzelas are not allowed.
- Lastly, only guide and assistance dogs with proper paperwork are allowed in Disneyland Paris. This rule keeps everyone safe and ensures the animals are taken care of properly.

Accessibility Information For Special Guests

As someone who understands the importance of ensuring that all guests have a magical and inclusive experience at Disneyland Paris, I want to provide you with valuable accessibility information for guests with physical disabilities, visual impairment and hearing impairment. Whether you're exploring the wonders of Disneyland Park or experiencing the magic of Walt Disney Studios Park, there are accommodations in place to ensure that everyone can fully enjoy their visit.

1. Guests With Physical Disabilities

When it comes to enjoying the attractions, Disneyland Paris has made efforts to ensure that everyone can experience the magic. For guests who may have difficulty moving from their wheelchair to a ride, select attractions have transfer boards available. These boards make it easier to board and exit the rides safely.

Moreover, some attractions have special vehicles designed to accommodate guests who prefer to remain in their wheelchairs throughout the experience. These vehicles allow for seamless boarding and exiting without the need to transfer to a different seat.

Moving around the parks and enjoying the various amenities is made easier with wheelchair accessibility in mind. All theaters, boutiques, and restaurants within Disneyland Paris are accessible by wheelchair, ensuring that guests can fully participate in shows, shop for souvenirs, and enjoy dining experiences without barriers.

For guests arriving by car, designated parking spaces are available specifically for those with disabilities. This ensures convenient access to the parks and facilities.

If you don't have your own wheelchair but require one during your visit, wheelchair rentals are available at Disneyland Paris. This service allows you to explore the parks comfortably at your own pace.

When nature calls, accessible restrooms are scattered throughout the parks to ensure that guests with disabilities have convenient access to facilities.

Disneyland Paris understands the importance of privacy and dignity for guests with limited mobility. That's why private changing rooms are available for those who need assistance or space to accommodate their needs comfortably.

2. Guests With Visual Impairment

For visitors who have trouble seeing, Disneyland Paris has some helpful tools to make their visit more enjoyable. One of these tools is the AudioSpot mobile app, which you can easily get for free on iPhones and Android phones. With this app, you can listen to descriptions of many rides and attractions in the parks. This helps people who are visually impaired to get into the stories and magic of Disney. Also, guide and assistance dogs are warmly welcomed everywhere in Disneyland Paris – on rides, in restaurants, and in shops. These furry friends give important help and companionship to visitors who have trouble seeing, so they can move around the parks confidently.

If you're visually impaired, you can find tactile and audio maps at the Guest Services desks in both Disneyland Park and Walt Disney Studios Park. These maps let you feel the layout of the park and get to know where the different attractions, places to eat, and facilities are. Plus, the audio part of these maps gives you spoken directions and descriptions, which makes the parks even easier to navigate. You can also get these maps online in PDF form before you visit, so you're prepared.

3. Guests With Hearing Impairment

For visitors who have trouble hearing, Disneyland Paris has special things to make sure they have a great time too. One thing they offer is shows in French Sign Language, usually on Saturday and Sunday afternoons. These shows let people who are deaf or hard of hearing experience the magic of Disney through visual storytelling and sign language.

They also have accessibility maps in English and French, showing where all the accessible facilities are in the parks. These maps point out wheelchair-friendly rides, restrooms, and restaurants, so visitors who have trouble hearing can move around the parks easily and confidently.

4. Guests with Other Forms of Disabilities

It's important to know that some attractions in Disneyland Paris may have flashing lights or other visual effects. While these elements add to the magic and excitement of the park for many people, they can be difficult for guests with epilepsy or sensitivity to lights. These effects might cause seizures or other health problems for individuals with these conditions.

To deal with these concerns, Disneyland Paris gives out maps that provide important information for guests with disabilities. These maps are very helpful, showing where all the accessible facilities in the parks are. This includes rides that are accessible for wheelchairs, restrooms, and restaurants, making sure that guests can move around the park easily.

Furthermore, the accessibility maps go even further by showing which attractions might have flashing lights or other visual effects that could cause health problems for guests with epilepsy or sensitivity to lights. This proactive approach helps guests to make smart choices about their park visit, so they can plan accordingly.

If you're worried about these issues, I really suggest looking at the accessibility maps before you go to Disneyland Paris. By checking out this important resource, you can find possible triggers and plan different routes or experiences to have a safe and fun visit.

Besides the accessibility maps, Disneyland Paris is dedicated to helping and supporting guests with disabilities throughout their visit. The park staff are trained to help people with different needs, and there are special Guest Relations spots where you can get more information and help.

Disneyland Paris offers things like special passes or specific viewing areas for shows and attractions, so that all guests can fully enjoy what the park has to offer. These options are meant to make the experience better for guests with disabilities, giving them the same chances to enjoy everything Disneyland Paris provides.

PLANNING YOUR VISIT

In this part, I'll guide you through all the information you need to make your trip easy. From grasping the park's opening times to discovering the ideal place to stay, I've got you covered.

Opening Hours

Let's discuss the operating hours at Disneyland Paris. It's pretty important information when you're planning your magical adventure, so let me explain it to you.

First of all, Disneyland Paris is open every day of the year, but here's the catch: the opening hours can change depending on the season. So, before you pack your bags and head off to meet Mickey and friends, make sure you check the opening times. Trust me, it'll save you from any unexpected surprises!

Now, let's dive into the details. Disneyland Park Paris usually starts the fun at 9:30 in the morning and keeps the party going until 10 in the evening. Yep, that's right, you've got plenty of time to enjoy all the magic!

Over at Walt Disney Studios Park Paris, the schedule is quite similar. They open their gates at 9:30 am too, but they finish a bit earlier, around 9 pm. Don't worry, though, there's still plenty of time to experience all the excitement!

Now, here's a little extra tip for you: if you're staying at one of the Disneyland Paris hotels or if you're an annual pass holder, you're in luck! You get something called Extra Magic Time, which basically means you can enter the parks an hour before they officially open to the public. How cool is that? For Disneyland Park Paris, Extra Magic Time runs from 8:30 am to 9:30 am, and for Walt Disney Studios Park, it's the same deal. So, if you're eager to beat the crowds and get a head start on your Disney adventure, this is the way to go!

Oh, and let's not forget about Disney Village. This lively spot opens bright and early at 8 in the morning and stays open until the late hours of the night, usually around midnight or even 1 am. So, whether you're craving a delicious breakfast or looking to continue the fun after a long day at the parks, Disney Village has got you covered.

Remember to always double-check those times before you set off.

Location Of Disneyland Paris

You're all prepared for the amazing adventure, and you're headed to Disneyland Paris. Now, where exactly is this magical place? Well, let me tell you all about it.

Disneyland Paris stands grandly in Chessy, France. It's not just an ordinary theme park; it's a whole world of enjoyment and excitement ready to be explored. And guess what? It's not just one park but two! You've got Disneyland Park, where fairy tales come alive, and Walt Disney Studios Park, where you can enter the captivating world of movies and animation.

Now, if you're wondering about the location, here it is: Boulevard de Parc, 77700 Coupvray, France. Remember that because that's where the magic starts.

And hey, if you're trying to find it on the map, look for the Golf Paris Val d'Europe. It's one of the nearest landmarks to Disneyland Paris. So, if you're golfing or just passing by, you know you're getting closer to the enchantment.

Getting Your Tickets Ready

Let's discuss preparing your tickets for an amazing adventure at Disneyland Paris. Trust me, it's going to be awesome!

Just a heads up, I'll only be sharing the various ticket options here. To check out the most recent prices and availability, make sure to visit the official Disneyland Paris website.

1. Hotel and Tickets Package

First, if you're looking for convenience and a touch of magic all in one, you might want to consider grabbing a Hotel and Ticket package. So, what's the deal with these packages? Well, when you choose a Hotel and Tickets offer with Disneyland Paris, you're in for a treat. You'll have access to both Disney Parks every day of your visit, and let me tell you, that's a lot of fun packed into one trip! Plus, you'll be staying at a fantastic Disney-themed hotel right by the parks. Talk about convenient!

Now, let's talk about the perks. Ever heard of Extra Magic Time? It's like a special pass to even more fun! With Extra Magic Time, you get to enter the Disney Parks before they officially open to the public. That means you can beat the crowds and get a head start on all the magic. Oh, and here's a little bonus: you'll also get to meet some of your favorite Disney characters during exclusive encounters at the hotel. Pretty cool, right?

2. Disney Park Tickets

Alright, now let's say you're more of a free spirit and prefer to go with just the park tickets. No worries, they've got you covered there too! With park tickets in hand, you'll have access to all the magic Disneyland Paris has to offer. That means you can enjoy all the attractions, watch all the shows, and even take some selfies with your favorite Disney characters at designated Selfie Spots. Talk about making memories!

But wait, there's more! When it comes to park tickets, you've got choices. You can choose to explore just one park – whether it's the classic Disneyland Park or the thrilling Walt Disney Studios Park – or you can go all out and experience both. The choice is yours! Plus, these tickets come with flexible conditions. Dated tickets can be canceled up to 3 days before your arrival, while undated tickets are valid for a whole year. Now that's what I call flexibility!

And hey, we haven't forgotten about the little ones. Kids aged 3 to 11 can enjoy special rates on tickets, making it even more affordable for the whole family to join in on the fun. And guess what? Children under 3 get in for free! So no need to worry about breaking the bank – Disneyland Paris has something for everyone.

3. Disneyland Pass

Bronze Pass: This pass gives you flexibility with payment options. You can choose to pay €18 per month for 11 months after an initial payment of €91, or opt for a single payment of €289 per year. With the Bronze Pass, you'll enjoy unlimited access to both Disney Parks on 170 days throughout the year, along with free parking.

Silver Pass: For a bit more access and perks, consider the Silver Pass. It costs €30 per month for 11 months after an initial payment of €169, or a single payment of €499 per year. With the Silver Pass, you'll have unlimited access to both Disney Parks on 300 days per year, free parking, and additional benefits like a 10% discount in Disneyland Paris shops and restaurants, as well as a 10% discount off Disney Annual PhotoPass.

Gold Pass: If you're looking for the ultimate Disney experience, the Gold Pass is the way to go. Priced at €45 per month for 11 months after an initial payment of €204, or a single payment of €699 per year, the Gold Pass provides boundless entry to both Disney Parks, complimentary parking, a 15% discount at Disneyland Paris shops and eateries, along with the added perk of a complimentary Annual PhotoPass and Extra.

Why buy a Disneyland Pass?

- Get to know the Disney Parks like the back of your hand: With unlimited access on select days, you'll have plenty of opportunities to explore every corner of Disneyland Paris.
- Discover Disneyland Paris throughout the seasons: Experience the magic of Disney in different seasons and enjoy seasonal events and attractions.
- Come for the day or just a few hours: Whether you're planning a full-day adventure or just popping in for a few hours of fun, a Disneyland Pass offers flexibility for your schedule.
- Benefit from discounts and exclusive advantages: Enjoy discounts on shopping, dining, and photo services, along with other exclusive perks.

How to buy a Disneyland Pass?

Purchasing your Disneyland Pass is easy and convenient. You can buy it through the following options:

- At the Disneyland Pass ticket offices: Located at the entrance of Walt Disney Studios Park, you can visit the ticket offices to purchase your pass directly.
- By placing a call: Simply dial +33 1 60 30 60 53 to speak with one of the Guest Relations team. They will assist you in purchasing your pass over the phone.

If you choose to buy your pass at the ticket office, it will be valid from the day of purchase. However, if you opt for purchasing over the phone, a voucher will be sent to you by post.

This voucher must be exchanged for your final Disneyland Pass at the ticket offices within 2 months of purchase. Once exchanged, your pass will be valid from the date of exchange.

Keep in mind that availability may be limited, so it's best to purchase your Disneyland Pass as soon as possible to ensure you can enjoy all the magic Disneyland Paris has to offer.

4. Special rate tickets

Now let me guide you through the process of getting your discounted tickets, especially if you or someone in your group has a disability.

Discounted Tickets for Special Needs:

If you or someone in your group has a disability, Disneyland Paris offers discounted tickets to make your visit easier and more enjoyable. With an official document showing the disability on the day of your visit, you can get a 25% discount on a 1-day/1-Park or a 1-day/2-Park Ticket.

But there's more – your companion also gets a 25% discount on their ticket if they provide an official document proving the disability. This means everyone in your group can enjoy the magic of Disneyland Paris without worrying about the cost.

Discounted Rates for Disneyland Pass:

If you want to stay longer and visit the parks multiple times, Disneyland Paris offers discounted rates on Disneyland Passes too. With an official document showing the disability, you can get a 25% discount on a Disneyland Pass. This gives you unlimited access to fun and adventure, so you can enjoy your favorite attractions as many times as you want.

Where to Get Your Discounted Tickets:

Now that you're excited about these discounts, let's talk about how and where to buy your tickets or passes. You can only get discounted tickets and annual passes at the special ticket offices near the entrance to the Disney Parks. Look for Counter 2 in Disneyland Park or Counter 1 in Walt Disney Studios Park to get your discounts.

If you're staying at one of the Disney Hotels, you can also buy your tickets or passes at the concierge desk. Just remember to bring an official document from your local government or medical authorities confirming the disability. A medical certificate alone won't be enough.

It's important to know that you don't have to book your tickets in advance to enter the Disney Parks. Just show your discounted tickets or passes at the entrance, and you can start enjoying the magic of Disneyland Paris right away.

Overview Of Accommodation Options

When planning your exciting trip to Disneyland Paris, one of the first things to think about is where to stay. Let me guide you through the lodging options, both Disney Hotels located on-site and rentals off-site, to assist you in making the best decision for your journey.

1. On-site Disneyland Paris Hotels

Let's begin with the Disney Hotels located on-site. These hotels offer various amenities and immersive experiences that complement your visit to the parks.

- ➢ Disney's Santa Fe Hotel: Tucked away in a vibrant, Southwestern-themed environment, Disney's Santa Fe Hotel provides a snug retreat for guests. The hotel features rooms inspired by Disney's Pixar movie "Cars," creating a lively setting for families. Amenities include a large swimming pool, complimentary shuttle service to the parks, a buffet-style restaurant serving Tex-Mex cuisine, and a souvenir shop.
- ➢ Disney's Cheyenne Hotel: Enter the Wild West ambiance at Disney's Cheyenne Hotel, where cowboy-themed lodgings await. The hotel's rustic allure and frontier-inspired decorations transport guests to another era. Amenities include a themed buffet-style restaurant, a play area for children, pony rides for little ones, and evening entertainment at the Red Garter Saloon.

- **Disney's Sequoia Lodge Hotel:** Drawing inspiration from nature, Disney's Sequoia Lodge Hotel offers a peaceful retreat surrounded by towering pine trees and rustic charm. Guests can relax in comfortable lodge rooms or enjoy the indoor and outdoor swimming pools, sauna, and whirlpool bath. The hotel also features a buffet-style restaurant serving hearty American dishes and a lounge bar with a cozy fireplace.
- **Disney's Newport Bay Club:** Embrace the maritime atmosphere at Disney's Newport Bay Club, an elegant waterfront hotel with scenic views of Lake Disney. The hotel showcases refined nautical decor, spacious rooms with maritime accents, and breathtaking views of the lake or gardens. Amenities include an indoor and outdoor pool complex, fitness center, upscale dining restaurant, and character breakfast experiences.
- **Disney's Hotel New York:** Immerse yourself in the vibrant ambiance of the Big Apple at Disney's Hotel New York, inspired by the iconic city skyline. The hotel offers chic rooms with modern decor, featuring artwork celebrating Marvel superheroes. Guests can savor fine dining at Manhattan Restaurant, unwind at the indoor pool and sauna, or explore the hotel's art gallery showcasing Marvel artwork.

- **Disneyland Hotel:** Serving as the pinnacle of luxury at Disneyland Paris, Disneyland Hotel offers unmatched comfort and convenience just moments away from the parks' entrance. The hotel emanates Victorian opulence with its majestic facade and luxurious interiors. Guests can indulge in gourmet dining at California Grill, relax at the Celestia Spa, and enjoy exclusive benefits like VIP FastPass access and character meet-and-greets.

2. **Off-site Hotels (First Options):**

While there are many great on-site hotels to stay at Disneyland Paris, renting a place off-site can also be a good option. It's often convenient, comfortable, and can even save you money. Let me walk you through some off-site accommodation options near Disneyland Paris.

- **Campanile Val De France Hotel:** Just a short distance from Disneyland Paris, the Campanile Val De France Hotel offers a convenient and comfy stay for visitors. It's in Magny-le-Hongre and has modern rooms with everything you need, like free Wi-Fi, air conditioning, and flat-screen TVs. Guests can enjoy a tasty buffet breakfast before heading out to Disneyland. Plus, the hotel has a restaurant serving different kinds of food, which makes dining easy for guests.

- **Dream Castle Hotel:** Set in a peaceful spot close to Disneyland Paris, the Dream Castle Hotel gives guests a fairy-tale experience. Inspired by medieval castles, this charming hotel has spacious rooms with luxurious furniture. Guests can relax in the hotel's spa or swim in the indoor pool. With perks like a free shuttle to the Disney parks and a yummy continental breakfast buffet, Dream Castle Hotel ensures a magical stay for visitors.

- **Explorers Hotel:** Perfect for families seeking adventure, the Explorers Hotel is just a few minutes from Disneyland Paris. This hotel has a pirate theme and rooms designed to spark the imagination of guests of all ages. Kids will love the indoor water playground with slides, while adults can relax in the sauna or gym. With free breakfast and evening entertainment, Explorers Hotel promises a memorable stay for the whole family.

- **Grand Magic Hotel:** In the heart of Val d'Europe, the Grand Magic Hotel offers a charming getaway for Disneyland Paris visitors. It has nicely decorated rooms with modern comforts like free Wi-Fi and flat-screen TVs. Guests can enjoy breakfast before exploring nearby attractions. With its great location and cozy vibe,

Grand Magic Hotel feels like a home away from home for travelers.

➢ **B&B Hotel:** Near Disneyland Paris, B&B Hotel offers affordable and comfortable accommodation. The hotel has cozy rooms with free Wi-Fi, comfy beds, and private bathrooms. Guests can enjoy a continental breakfast before heading to Disneyland. With its reasonable rates and convenient location, B&B Hotel is a smart choice for making the most of your Disneyland experience.

3. **Offsite Hotels (Second Options):**

➢ **Relais Spa Chessy Val D'Europe:** Located in the lovely town of Chessy, just a short distance from Disneyland Paris, Relais Spa Chessy Val D'Europe offers luxurious stays for guests seeking relaxation and indulgence. The hotel has large suites with modern amenities, including fully equipped kitchens and private balconies. Guests can relax at the hotel's spa and wellness center, which includes a sauna, steam room, and indoor pool. With its classy atmosphere and convenient location, Relais Spa Chessy Val D'Europe is the perfect getaway after a day of fun at Disneyland.

- **Adagio Serris Val D'Europe:** Next to the Val d'Europe shopping center and only a few minutes from Disneyland Paris, Adagio Serris Val D'Europe provides comfortable and convenient stays for travelers. The hotel offers roomy apartments with fully equipped kitchens, making it a great option for families or longer stays. Guests can enjoy amenities such as a fitness center, laundry facilities, and free Wi-Fi. With its central location and homey comforts, Adagio Serris Val D'Europe offers a peaceful escape for visitors to Disneyland Paris.
- **Moxy Paris Val D'Europe:** Located in the heart of Val d'Europe, Moxy Paris Val D'Europe offers a trendy and lively atmosphere for guests. The hotel has stylishly designed rooms with modern amenities, including smart TVs and USB outlets. Guests can relax in the hotel's common areas, which include a 24/7 bar and lounge. With its convenient location near Disneyland Paris and affordable rates, Moxy Paris Val D'Europe is a great choice for travelers seeking comfort and convenience.
- **Vallee Val D'Europe:** Conveniently situated within walking distance of Disneyland Paris, Vallee Val D'Europe offers cozy accommodation for visitors to the theme parks. The hotel has comfortable rooms with

amenities such as free Wi-Fi, flat-screen TVs, and mini-fridges. Guests can enjoy a continental breakfast buffet before heading out to explore Disneyland. With its helpful staff and convenient location, Vallee Val D'Europe provides a pleasant stay for travelers.

- **Hotel L'Elysee Val D'Europe:** Situated in the heart of Val d'Europe, Hotel L'Elysee Val D'Europe offers a friendly atmosphere for guests visiting Disneyland Paris. The hotel has spacious rooms decorated in a modern style, with amenities such as free Wi-Fi and flat-screen TVs. Guests can enjoy a tasty breakfast buffet at the hotel's dining area before starting their Disneyland adventure. With its convenient location and comfortable rooms, Hotel L'Elysee Val D'Europe is a fantastic choice for travelers seeking a memorable Disneyland experience.

- **Adagio Marne La Vallee Val D'Europe:** Just a short distance from Disneyland Paris, Adagio Marne La Vallee Val D'Europe provides modern and spacious accommodation for guests. The hotel offers well-equipped apartments with kitchenettes, making it an ideal choice for families or longer stays. Guests can make use of amenities such as a fitness center, laundry facilities, and free Wi-Fi. With its convenient location and comfortable amenities, Adagio Marne La Vallee Val D'Europe offers a relaxing retreat for visitors to Disneyland Paris.

Each of these hotels located both on-site and off-site has its own special appeal and features, designed to meet different tastes and budgets. Whether you're looking for luxury, convenience, or affordability, you're certain to discover the ideal place to stay for your enchanting vacation near Disneyland Paris. For the latest prices and availability, make sure to visit the official websites of these hotels.

Booking Tips And Considerations

Let me share some insider tips and considerations to help you find the perfect place to stay for your trip.

- First, let's talk about timing. Booking your stay well ahead can save you a lot of money and make sure you have a nice place to sleep after a day at Disney. Especially during busy times like holidays or Halloween, rooms fill up quickly. So, it's smart to reserve your spot as soon as you know your travel dates.

- When choosing where to stay, there are a few important things to think about. First, consider your budget. Decide how much you can afford for your stay and stick to it. Remember, you'll want to have money left for souvenirs and snacks at the parks.
- Next, think about your travel style and what you like. Do you like getting up early to go on rides, or do you prefer to take your time? If you're an early riser, it might be worth spending more to stay close to the parks. But if you like staying up late, a cozy place away from the parks might be better.
- Accessibility is also important, especially if you or someone with you has trouble moving around. Many hotels offer rooms and facilities for people with mobility issues, but it's a good idea to check and talk to the hotel before booking.
- Don't forget to read reviews and do some research. Websites like TripAdvisor and Booking.com have lots of honest reviews from other travelers. Look for comments about cleanliness, service, and overall experience to make sure you're choosing the best place for your trip.
- Finally, go with your instincts. If a place feels right and has everything you need, go for it! Your accommodation

sets the mood for your whole trip, so it's important to pick somewhere you'll feel comfortable and happy.

GETTING TO DISNEYLAND PARIS

Getting to Disneyland Paris and understanding its facilities is essential for a smooth and enjoyable visit. When planning your trip, it's crucial to know how to reach the magical destination and what amenities are available once you arrive. In this section, I'll guide you through transportation options, parking details, and the facilities provided on-site. Let's ensure your journey to Disneyland Paris is as hassle-free as possible.

Transportation Options

When it comes to reaching Disneyland Paris, you have various transportation choices, each with its own advantages and things to think about. Let me explain it to you.

Public Transportation

➢ **By Plane/Bus:**

If you're in central Paris, catching a bus to Disneyland Paris is easy. The Disneyland Paris Express buses are a handy choice, leaving from important places like Gare du Nord, Eiffel Tower, Opera, and Chatelet bus stations. They run many times in the morning, and you can buy your bus tickets online when you buy your Disneyland Paris entry tickets. These buses take you to the magic in about an hour, giving you a comfy journey without the trouble of driving. Also, if you're flying into Orly Airport or Charles de Gaulle Airport, the Magical Shuttle buses are available, leaving every hour for Disneyland Paris.

- ➢ By Train:

For a fast and effective ride, the RER Line A is your way to Disneyland Paris. Just get on at any RER station and go towards Marne-la-Vallée/Chessy station, which is only a short walk from the theme parks and Disney Village. Trains come every 15 minutes, making it simple to catch one no matter where you are in Paris. And if you're coming from Charles de Gaulle Airport, think about taking a TGV train for a quick journey to the magic.

- ➢ By Eurostar Trains:

Traveling from London? Eurostar trains offer a smooth trip to Disneyland Paris. Get on at St Pancras International and get off at Marne-la-Vallée - Chessy station, just a few steps from the parks. With direct trains leaving several times a week, it's a handy choice for UK visitors.

Alternatively, you can take a Eurostar to Lille and switch to a TGV train heading for Disneyland Paris.

Private Car

For those who like the freedom of their own car, driving to Disneyland Paris is easy. From Paris, just follow the signs for the 'Paris' mark if you're coming from the South, or 'Metz / Nancy' if you're coming from the North. Exit 14 will take you straight to the parks or Disneyland hotels. And if you're coming from the UK, the Eurotunnel offers a smooth trip from Folkestone to Calais, followed by a scenic drive to Disneyland Paris. Alternatively, you can choose a ferry ride from Calais, with Disneyland Paris just a few hours' drive away.

> Parking Facilities:

Parking at Disneyland Paris is easy, with free parking available at select Disneyland hotels for guests staying on-site. Just show your check-in card to access the parking facilities without hassle. For day visitors and those staying off-site, convenient parking lots are close to the parks and Disney Village, offering easy access for a fee of €30.

So whether you like the convenience of public transportation or the freedom of your own car, getting to Disneyland Paris is simple!

Overview Of On-Site Facilities

Alright, let's take a look at the overview of the facilities available at Disneyland Paris. From bathrooms to places for taking care of babies, and even places for medical assistance, Disneyland Paris has everything you need for a comfortable and worry-free visit.

> Restrooms:

One of the most important things to consider when visiting any theme park is restroom availability. You'll be happy to know that Disneyland Paris has many restrooms conveniently located throughout the parks. Whether you're exploring Disneyland Park or Walt Disney Studios, you'll always find a clean and well-maintained restroom nearby. These restrooms are regularly cleaned and stocked to ensure a pleasant experience for guests of all ages.

> Medical Facilities:

Safety is a big concern at Disneyland Paris, and part of that is making sure there are medical facilities available for guests who need them. You'll find First Aid Kits easily accessible at various locations throughout the parks. These kits contain essential supplies for dealing with minor injuries or sicknesses that might happen during your visit. Additionally, Automated External Defibrillators (AEDs) are placed strategically in important areas for quick access in case of medical emergencies.

> Baby Care Facilities:

Traveling with young children? Disneyland Paris knows that families with babies and toddlers have special needs. That's why they offer special centers where parents can take care of their little ones in a comfortable and private space. These centers have changing tables, rooms for nursing, places for feeding, and even supplies like diapers and baby wipes available for purchase. Also, if you don't want to bring your own stroller, you can rent one for added convenience.

> Other Facilities:

Besides restrooms, medical facilities, and baby care centers, Disneyland Paris offers a few other things to make your visit better:

Water Fountains: Stay hydrated during your day at the park with water fountains conveniently placed around the parks. You can refill your water bottle or have a quick drink to stay refreshed and energized.

Free Wi-Fi: Stay connected and share your magical moments with friends and family thanks to free Wi-Fi available throughout Disneyland Paris. Whether you're checking ride wait times or posting photos on social media, staying connected is easy.

Phone Charging Stations: Don't let a low battery slow you down! Keep your devices charged and ready for action with designated phone charging stations located throughout the parks. Whether you need to charge your phone or camera, these convenient stations ensure you never miss a photo opportunity or important communication.

THEME PARKS

*A*s we start on this journey together, I'm excited to introduce you to the essence of the Disneyland Paris experience: the captivating theme parks of Disneyland Park and Walt Disney Studios.

These two parks are the lively center of Disneyland Paris, each offering its own special mix of excitement, amazement, and creativity. From the famous fairy tale castle of Disneyland Park to the magic happening behind the scenes at Walt Disney Studios, there's something for every visitor to find and enjoy.

In this part of the travel guide, we'll explore the charming attractions, captivating shows, and enjoyable experiences waiting for you in both Disneyland Park and Walt Disney Studios.

Whether you're looking for thrilling adventures, delightful encounters with beloved characters, or simply the fun of exploring imaginative worlds, these theme parks are sure to leave you enchanted.

Disneyland Park & Walt Disney Studios

As you step into Disneyland Paris, get ready to dive into a magical world full of wonder and excitement. Allow me to walk you through the enchanting lands of Disneyland Park and Walt Disney Studios, where the magic happens right before your eyes.

Disneyland Park Paris

Let's begin with Disneyland Park, the core of Disneyland Paris. Opened in 1992, this famous park was initially called EuroDisney until May 1994. Changing its name to Disneyland Paris was a strategic decision to capture the charming essence of France, filled with romance and allure. The shift from "Euro" was intentional, as it brought to mind business and trade rather than the magical allure of Disney.

Crafted by the renowned Walt Disney Imagineering, Disneyland Park captivates visitors with its detailed layout reminiscent of California's Disneyland Park and Florida's Magic Kingdom Park. Spreading over 140 acres, it stands as the second-largest park in Disney's collection, following Shanghai Disneyland Park in size.

Disneyland Park Zones

As you wander through Disneyland Park, you'll discover a variety of themed areas, each offering its own special mix of attractions and adventures. Let's explore them together:

1. **Main Street USA:** Take a journey back to early 20th-century America as you walk along Main Street USA. Filled with charming shops, old-fashioned cars, and nostalgic tunes, this lively street sets the scene for your Disneyland adventure.
2. **Discoveryland:** Step into the future with Discoveryland, where imagination meets innovation. From the retro-futuristic design of Space Mountain to the steampunk-inspired wonders of Les Mystères du Nautilus, this area invites you to discover the marvels of tomorrow.
3. **Frontierland:** Gear up for excitement in Frontierland, where the essence of the Wild West comes alive. From thrilling rides like Big Thunder Mountain to immersive shows like the Legends of the Wild West, there's adventure waiting around every turn.

4. **Adventureland:** Embark on a journey of exploration in Adventureland, where exotic places and daring adventures await. Encounter swashbuckling pirates on Pirates of the Caribbean, brave the perilous jungles of Indiana Jones and the Temple of Peril, and set sail on the mysterious waters of Adventure Isle.
5. **Fantasyland:** Step into a world of magic and fairy tales in Fantasyland, where dreams come true for guests of all ages. From classic attractions like Peter Pan's Flight and It's a Small World to beloved Disney characters roaming the streets, there's enchantment at every corner.

Each of these areas offers its own unique atmosphere and attractions, ensuring there's something for everyone to enjoy at Disneyland Park.

So, whether you're exploring the untamed frontier, flying through the stars, or going on a magical adventure, Disneyland Park guarantees an unforgettable experience for the whole family.

Now, let's head over to Walt Disney Studios, where the enchantment of moviemaking takes the spotlight. But that's a tale for another part of our journey through Disneyland Paris.

Walt Disney Studio Park

Let's explore the Walt Disney Studios Park. Originally thought of as the Disney-MGM Studios Park, this park faced some money troubles before finally opening its doors on March 16, 2002. Since then, it has grown with various expansions to make the visitor experience better.

One big expansion happened in June 2007 when they added the Animation Courtyard. This part showed off the studio's long history of animation, with favorite characters and movie stuff. Visitors got to go on fun rides, meet characters, and buy unique stuff you can't find in other Disney parks.

In 2009, the park kept changing with new shows, like Playhouse Disney – Live on Stage! This lively show was in three languages and was fun for everyone. Also, Disney's Cinema Parade showed off the magic of favorite Disney movies with colorful floats and characters.

Jump ahead to 2018, and the park changed again for the 2024 summer Olympics. They spent a lot of money, 2 billion Euros, to make the park even better. They added cool themes from famous franchises like Marvel, Star Wars, and Frozen. Now you can pretend to be your favorite heroes, explore far-off galaxies, and visit the icy land of Arendelle – all at Walt Disney Studios Park.

Walt Disney Studios Park Zones

Now, let's look at the different parts of the park:

1. **Front Lot:** When you first come in, you're in the busy Front Lot. It's like being in Hollywood, with famous places and busy streets. This sets the scene for the adventures you'll have.
2. **Production Courtyard:** Here, you can see how movies are made behind the scenes. You can go on fun rides, learn about special effects, and maybe see your favorite Disney characters.
3. **Toon Studio:** This is where you can see classic Disney cartoons come to life with bright colors and fun designs. There are lots of exciting things to do for fans of animation.
4. **Worlds of Pixar:** This part is all about the amazing worlds from Pixar movies. You can follow Woody and Buzz on their adventures or join Nemo and Dory under the sea. It's a celebration of the characters and stories we all love.

As you explore Walt Disney Studios Park, you'll feel like you're in a world where dreams come true and there's wonder around every corner.

Detailed Guide To Rides And Attractions In Each Park

Let's explore a detailed guide to the rides and attractions in each park at Disneyland Paris. I'll take you through each exciting experience, starting with Disneyland Park.

Disneyland Park Paris Rides and Attractions

1. Star Tours: The Adventures Continue:

Embark on a space journey through the Star Wars universe aboard Star Tours: The Adventures Continue. Located in Discoveryland, this thrilling attraction takes you to different planets where you'll battle the Empire. Suitable for adventurers of all ages, this ride promises an unforgettable experience.

2. Big Thunder Mountain:

Feel the excitement as you speed through a mine on a runaway train aboard Big Thunder Mountain. Located in Frontierland, this high-speed adventure is perfect for thrill-seekers of all ages. Hold on tight as you twist and turn through the rugged terrain, encountering surprises along the way.

3. Phantom Manor:

Get ready to be spooked as you enter Phantom Manor, located in Frontierland. This dark ride takes you on a chilling journey through a haunted mansion, where ghosts and spirits lurk around every corner. Suitable for adults, teens, and tweens, Phantom Manor offers a hauntingly memorable experience.

4. Thunder Mesa Riverboat Landing:

For a relaxing cruise along the Rivers of America, hop aboard the Thunder Mesa Riverboat Landing in Frontierland. This scenic boat ride offers beautiful views of the park's landmarks, making it perfect for guests of all ages seeking a tranquil escape.

5. Blanche-Neige et les Sept Nains:

Join Snow White and the Seven Dwarfs on a magical journey through the forest aboard Blanche-Neige et les Sept Nains in

Fantasyland. Encounter the Evil Queen and other beloved characters in this enchanting ride suitable for guests of all ages.

6. *Casey Jr. – le Petit Train du Cirque:*

Experience the fun of the circus as you ride aboard Casey Jr. – le Petit Train du Cirque in Fantasyland. This delightful train ride takes you through the circus grounds, where you'll see clowns, acrobats, and other performers. Perfect for guests of all ages, this ride offers fun for the whole family.

7. *Dumbo the Flying Elephant:*

Fly through the skies aboard Dumbo the Flying Elephant in Fantasyland. Enjoy breathtaking views of Fantasyland as you ride atop Dumbo's back, making this attraction perfect for guests of all ages seeking a magical experience.

8. *Pirates of the Caribbean:*

Embark on a pirate adventure aboard Pirates of the Caribbean in Adventureland. Sail the high seas, battle pirates, and explore a haunted bayou and cursed town in this thrilling attraction suitable for guests of all ages.

9. *Pirates' Beach:*

Relax on the sandy shores of Pirates' Beach in Adventureland. Take in views of the castle and enjoy a moment of peace in this serene setting, perfect for kids looking to take a break from the excitement of the park.

10. Adventure Isle:

Explore a lost world of dinosaurs and pirates on Adventure Isle in Adventureland. Discover hidden caves, cross rickety bridges, and uncover ancient ruins in this thrilling land suitable for adventurers of all ages.

11. Le Passage Enchanté d'Aladdin:

Enter the enchanting world of Aladdin and Jasmine aboard Le Passage Enchanté d'Aladdin in Adventureland. Meet the Genie, ride the magic carpet, and embark on a whimsical journey through Agrabah in this delightful attraction suitable for guests of all ages.

12. Autopia:

Race around a track in electric cars aboard Autopia in Discoveryland. Whether you're up for a competitive race or a leisurely drive through the countryside, this attraction offers fun for guests of all ages.

13. Buzz Lightyear Laser Blast:

Join Buzz Lightyear on a mission to save the galaxy aboard Buzz Lightyear Laser Blast in Discoveryland. Blast your way through space, defeat Zurg, and become a hero in this action-packed attraction suitable for guests of all ages.

14. Mickey's PhilharMagic:

Dive into a 4D musical journey with Mickey and his friends aboard Mickey's PhilharMagic in Discoveryland. Travel through worlds inspired by Disney movies and experience the magic of music in this enchanting attraction suitable for guests of all ages.

15. Orbitron:

Take a spin through the galaxy aboard Orbitron in Discoveryland. Spin and twirl in a giant space station as you explore the cosmos and meet friendly aliens in this out-of-this-world attraction suitable for guests of all ages.

16. The Sleeping Beauty Gallery:

Step into the enchanting world of Sleeping Beauty as you visit The Sleeping Beauty Gallery. Located in Fantasyland, this exhibit allows you to immerse yourself in the timeless tale of Sleeping Beauty.

Marvel at the majestic castle and meet the fairies as they guide you through the story. Perfect for visitors of all ages, this experience is sure to leave you spellbound.

17. The Dragon's Lair:

Venture into the depths of Fantasyland and discover the hidden secrets of The Dragon's Lair. Encounter a friendly dragon as you explore this mystical cavern filled with treasures untold. Whether you're young or young at heart, this adventure is sure to ignite your imagination and leave you with memories to treasure.

18. Lancelot's Carousel:

Join knights and princesses on a magical journey aboard Lancelot's Carousel. Located in Fantasyland, this enchanting carousel promises a delightful experience for all ages. Take a spin and immerse yourself in a world of fantasy and adventure as you create cherished memories with your loved ones.

19. The Land of Fairy Tales:

Embark on a whimsical journey through The Land of Fairy Tales in Fantasyland. Meet beloved characters and explore a magical forest filled with wonder and enchantment. Suitable for visitors of all ages, The Land of Fairy Tales offers a delightful experience that will captivate your imagination and leave you longing for more.

20. Gardens of Wonder:

Experience the magic of Disneyland Paris' 30th Anniversary celebration at the Gardens of Wonder. Admire 30 unique statues of beloved Disney characters, specially crafted for this milestone occasion. Located in Main Street USA, this enchanting garden is a must-visit for guests of all ages.

21. Horse-drawn Streetcars:

Take a leisurely ride down Main Street USA aboard a charming horse-drawn streetcar. Enjoy the sights and sounds of Disneyland Paris as you learn about its rich history and heritage. Suitable for visitors of all ages, this nostalgic experience offers a delightful way to explore the park.

22. Liberty Arcade:

Immerse yourself in American history at Liberty Arcade, located in Main Street USA. Engage in interactive exhibits and games that bring the past to life. Suitable for visitors of all ages, this educational experience is both entertaining and enlightening.

23. Main Street Vehicles:

Step back in time and experience the charm of Main Street USA aboard vintage vehicles. Whether you choose a horse-drawn carriage or a classic car, this nostalgic ride promises a journey filled with magic and wonder. Suitable for visitors of all ages, Main Street Vehicles offer a unique way to explore Disneyland Paris.

24. Meet Mickey Mouse:

No visit to Disneyland Paris is complete without meeting the one and only Mickey Mouse! Head to Fantasyland to greet Mickey and his pals, snap a photo, and collect autographs. Suitable for visitors of all ages, this magical encounter is sure to be a highlight of your trip.

25. Princess Pavilion:

Enter the Princess Pavilion in Fantasyland and meet Disney's beloved princesses. Listen to their enchanting stories, pose for photos, and collect autographs. Suitable for visitors of all ages, this royal encounter promises to make you feel like royalty.

26. Peter Pan's Flight:

Join Peter Pan on a high-flying adventure to Neverland! Located in Fantasyland, Peter Pan's Flight allows you to soar over London and embark on a magical journey filled with excitement and wonder. Suitable for visitors of all ages, this classic attraction is a must-visit for Disney fans.

27. Sleeping Beauty Castle:

Marvel at the iconic Sleeping Beauty Castle, a symbol of magic and enchantment at Disneyland Paris. Located in Fantasyland, this majestic castle invites you to explore its enchanting surroundings and learn about its rich history. Suitable for visitors of all ages, a visit to Sleeping Beauty Castle is sure to leave you feeling inspired.

28. Discovery Arcade:

Journey through Disney history at Discovery Arcade, located in Main Street USA. Explore interactive exhibits and games that celebrate the legacy of Disneyland Paris. Suitable for visitors of all ages, this immersive experience offers a fascinating glimpse into the magic behind the scenes.

29. Disneyland Railroad:

Climb aboard the Disneyland Railroad and embark on a scenic journey around the park. Sit back, relax, and take in the sights as you learn about the history and heritage of Disneyland Paris.

Suitable for visitors of all ages, this leisurely ride is a wonderful way to explore the park and create lasting memories.

30. Mad Hatter's Tea Cups:

Enter the magical realm of Alice in Wonderland and hop aboard the Mad Hatter's Tea Party! Jump into a big teacup and brace yourself for an exciting journey as you whirl and twirl to cheerful music.

Situated in Fantasyland, this timeless ride is ideal for visitors of any age. Whether you love excitement or prefer a gentler experience, the Mad Hatter's Tea Cups provide enjoyment for everyone in the family.

From enchanting fairy tales to thrilling adventures, Disneyland Park Paris offers a diverse array of rides and attractions that promise fun and excitement for visitors of all ages.

Whether you're exploring Fantasyland or strolling down Main Street USA, each experience is sure to leave you with cherished memories that will last a lifetime. So, come and discover the magic of Disneyland Park Paris – where dreams really do come true!

Walt Disney Studio Park Attractions

1. RC Racer:

Imagine being in the driver's seat of an exciting RC car, zooming along a half-pipe track with twists and turns that will leave you breathless. That's exactly what you'll experience at RC Racer! This fast ride takes you on a wild journey as you soar up and down the towering track, feeling the rush of excitement with every twist and turn.

Whether you're someone who loves excitement or just looking for some heart-pounding fun, RC Racer is sure to provide an unforgettable experience.

2. Cars Road Trip:

Get ready to hit the open road with Lightning McQueen and the gang on Cars Road Trip! Step into the world of Disney Pixar's Cars as you go on a scenic tour through Radiator Springs and beyond. From Mater's Junkyard Jamboree to Luigi's Casa Della Tires, you'll meet all your favorite characters and see iconic landmarks from the beloved film.

With engaging storytelling and beautiful scenery, Cars Road Trip is a ride that the whole family can enjoy.

3. *The Twilight Zone Tower of Terror:*

Prepare for a thrilling journey into the unknown aboard The Twilight Zone Tower of Terror. Take a nerve-wracking elevator ride through the eerie corridors of the Hollywood Tower Hotel, where you'll encounter ghostly apparitions and mysterious phenomena. With its thrilling drops and atmospheric storytelling, this iconic attraction is not for the faint of heart.

4. *Ratatouille: The Adventure:*

Join Remy the rat on a culinary adventure through Gusteau's kitchen in Ratatouille: The Adventure. Shrink down to the size of a rat and navigate through larger-than-life sets as you dodge obstacles and race through Parisian streets. With its innovative 3D technology and engaging storytelling, this delightful attraction is a must-see for fans of the beloved Pixar film.

5. *Rock 'n' Roller Coaster Starring Aerosmith:*

Get ready to rock out with Aerosmith on the high-speed Rock 'n' Roller Coaster. Strap in for a thrilling roller coaster experience set to the pulse-pounding beats of classic rock music. Zoom through loop-de-loops and corkscrew turns in the darkened concert venue, feeling the adrenaline rush as you soar through the night sky.

6. *Animation Academy:*

At the Animation Academy, unleash your inner artist and learn to draw beloved Disney characters under the guidance of experienced professionals. Located in Toon Studio, this activity is perfect for all ages. Whether you're an aspiring artist or just looking for a fun and creative experience, you'll enjoy bringing your favorite characters to life on paper and taking home your masterpiece as a cherished souvenir.

7. *Marvel Avengers Campus:*

Step into the action-packed world of Marvel at Avengers Campus. Join your favorite superheroes as they fight against evil forces in exciting attractions and immersive experiences. From meeting iconic characters to going on heroic missions, Marvel Avengers Campus offers excitement and adventure for fans of all ages.

8. *Crush's Coaster:*

Hang ten with Crush the sea turtle on Crush's Coaster, a wild spinning roller coaster adventure inspired by Disney Pixar's Finding Nemo. Climb aboard your turtle shell and ride the East Australian Current, twisting and turning through underwater tunnels and swirling whirlpools.

With its dynamic motion and immersive theming, this aquatic thrill ride is sure to make a splash with guests of all ages.

9. Toy Soldiers Parachute Drop:

Join the ranks of the Toy Story soldiers and experience the thrill of parachuting from a towering height. Board your parachute and prepare for a gentle descent as you enjoy panoramic views of Toy Story Playland below. This whimsical attraction is perfect for younger guests and offers a bird's-eye view of the colorful surroundings.

10. Cars Quatre Roues Rallye:

Rev your engines and race through the desert landscape of Radiator Springs on Cars Quatre Roues Rallye. Climb aboard your own race car and spin and swirl around tight turns and banked curves. With its family-friendly thrills and vibrant Cars-themed scenery, this attraction is sure to delight fans of all ages.

11. Disney Studio 1:

Step into the heart of Hollywood at Disney Studio 1, where movie magic comes to life in an immersive indoor setting. Stroll down Hollywood Boulevard and marvel at iconic landmarks and bustling street scenes straight out of Tinseltown. With its dazzling facades and hidden details, Disney Studio 1 is the perfect backdrop for capturing memorable photos and creating lasting memories.

From artistic adventures to thrilling rides, Walt Disney Studio Park offers a variety of attractions and experiences to suit every taste and preference.

Must-See Highlights And Hidden Gems

When it comes to Disneyland Paris, there's more than meets the eye. Sure, you've got your classic attractions and beloved characters, but let me take you on a journey beyond the usual sights. Let's uncover some must-see highlights and hidden gems that will make your trip truly unforgettable.

> *Disneyland Park Paris:*

Ah, Disneyland Park Paris, where dreams come to life! While everyone rushes to the big-name attractions, don't forget to slow down and savor the little details. One hidden gem you don't want to miss is the Disneyland Railroad (Paris). Picture this: a leisurely train ride aboard an authentic steam-powered locomotive, chugging along a 3 km route around the park. As you depart from Main Street U.S.A station, keep your eyes peeled for iconic sights like the Grand Canyon Diorama, Pirates of the Caribbean, and Indiana Jones and the Temple of Peril. It's a charming journey through Disney history that's sure to delight train enthusiasts and casual riders alike.

> *Walt Disney Studios Park:*

Over at Walt Disney Studios Park, adventure awaits around every corner. While the blockbuster attractions steal the spotlight, take a moment to explore the quieter corners of the park. One hidden gem that often gets overlooked is Golf Disneyland. Yes, you heard that right – a Disney-themed golf course! Nestled in Marne-La-Vallée, Golf Disneyland offers a picturesque setting for golfers of all skill levels. After a round on the greens, unwind at the clubhouse terrace restaurant or browse the pro shop for souvenirs. It's the perfect blend of relaxation and recreation, Disney style.

> *Disney Village:*

Now, let's talk about Disney Village, the bustling hub of dining, entertainment, and shopping just steps away from the parks. While the restaurants and shops draw crowds, there's a hidden gem tucked away in the heart of it all – Val d'Europe. This sprawling shopping mall, created by the Walt Disney Company, offers a diverse array of experiences for visitors.

From fashion boutiques to gastronomic delights, there's something for everyone here. Plus, with its own RER station connecting it to Paris and other Disneyland Paris resorts, it's easily accessible for a day of retail therapy.

> *Disneyland Paris Hotels:*

Of course, no trip to Disneyland Paris would be complete without a stay in one of its enchanting hotels. While the official hotels offer themed accommodations for every budget, there's a hidden gem waiting to be discovered – Villages Nature Paris by Center Parcs. This nature resort, nestled amidst lush greenery, offers a tranquil escape from the hustle and bustle of the parks. With aquatic activities, lakeside promenades, and sustainable accommodations, it's a refreshing change of pace for nature lovers.

> *Disneyland Paris Resorts:*

If you're craving even more adventure, why not venture beyond the parks to explore Disneyland Paris resorts? One hidden gem that promises an unforgettable experience is Disney's Davy Crockett Ranch. Tucked away in the woods like a scene from the American frontier, this rustic retreat offers cozy cabin accommodations and outdoor activities galore.

From swimming in the tropical pool to exploring the outdoor playground, it's a wild west adventure for the whole family.

> *Disneyland Paris Restaurants and Shops:*

And let's not forget about the dining and shopping experiences at Disneyland Paris. While the restaurants and shops within the parks offer plenty of magic, keep an eye out for hidden gems that offer unique flavors and treasures. Whether you're indulging in a gourmet meal at a themed restaurant or browsing for souvenirs at a boutique shop, every moment is a chance to discover something new and exciting.

So there you have it, my friends, a glimpse into the hidden gems of Disneyland Paris. Go ahead, venture off the beaten path and discover the magic that awaits around every corner.

Exploring Disney Village

Welcome to Disney Village, a magical center of entertainment and excitement tucked in Marne-la-Vallée, France, between the enchanting Disneyland Park, Walt Disney Studios Park, and the cozy Disney Hotels.

As your guide, let me take you on a journey through this lively city of wonder, where every corner is brimming with the spirit of adventure and fun.

Crafted by the famous architect Frank Gehry, Disney Village was imagined as a free-flowing area where visitors could dive into entertainment before or after their park adventures. The idea was to make an open, welcoming atmosphere lit up by gentle lights, like a starry night sky.

However, initial plans, using bits of an old power station, felt too chilly and industrial. To warm up the vibe, metal frames were swapped with charming statues and inviting food stands, turning Disney Village into a friendly retreat for visitors from around the world.

Originally called Festival Disney when it opened in 1992, Disney Village went through several changes over the years. In 1996, it got renamed as Disney Village, establishing itself as a lively entertainment spot.

With time, new attractions and experiences popped up, including famous places like Planet Hollywood and Rainforest Cafe, adding to the charm of this bustling city of dreams. Also, adding to the excitement, there were expansions in entertainment options, like the 570-seat IMAX cinema and PanoraMagique, one of the world's biggest tethered balloons.

Where is Disney Village located?

Situated conveniently between the parks and hotels, Disney Village is easy to reach for visitors staying at Disney Hotels. A free shuttle service runs between the hotels and Disney Village, offering an easy way to explore this magical place. Just hop on one of the shuttles, which leave every 12 minutes from 6:30 AM to 11 PM, and get ready for an adventure full of entertainment and joy.

For guests staying at Villages Nature Paris or other nearby places, public shuttle buses give easy access to Disney Village, making sure everyone can enjoy the magic of this enchanting spot.

Operating Hours:

Disney Village welcomes guests every day of the week, usually from 8 AM to 12 AM or 1 AM. However, it's always wise to check the official website for any updates or changes, especially during bad weather. Whether you're enjoying delicious dining, browsing lovely shops, or diving into thrilling entertainment, Disney Village guarantees endless enchantment from early morning till late at night.

Top Ways to Enjoy the Disney Village

➤ **Watch a Movie at the Cinemas**

Looking for some movie magic? Head over to the Disney Village Cinemas, where you can watch the latest hit movies on one of their 10 screens. Whether you're in the mood for action, adventure, or comedy, there's something for everyone here.

Shop at the World of Disney

For the ultimate Disney shopping experience, step into the World of Disney store. Here, you'll find a treasure trove of items inspired by your favorite Disney characters and stories. From clothes and accessories to toys and collectibles, this is the perfect place to buy souvenirs for yourself or gifts for loved ones back home.

➤ **Enjoy a Meal at the Rainforest Cafe**

Indulge your senses at the Rainforest Cafe, a restaurant with a tropical theme where dining meets adventure. As you enjoy delicious food, you'll be surrounded by lush plants, waterfalls, and animatronic animals that make the rainforest come to life. It's a dining experience unlike any other, sure to delight guests of all ages.

➤ **Experience Buffalo Bill's Wild West Show**

Get ready for an unforgettable journey back in time at Buffalo Bill's Wild West Show. This live performance takes you to the days of the Wild West, with cowboys, Indians, and thrilling stunts. Sit back and enjoy the show, as you witness a performance filled with action, music, and excitement.

> Play Games at the Arcade

Looking for some classic arcade fun? Head to the arcade in Disney Village, where you can test your skills and win prizes on a variety of games. Whether you're good at pinball or air hockey, there's plenty of entertainment here. It's the perfect way to relax and have some fun with family and friends.

> Take a Stroll Through the Gardens

After all the excitement, why not take a leisurely walk through the beautiful gardens of Disney Village? Enjoy the sights and sounds of nature as you walk along winding paths, surrounded by colorful flowers and lush greenery. It's a peaceful retreat from the hustle and bustle of the village, perfect for tired travelers.

GUIDE TO SHOWS, PARADES AND EVENTS

I n this part, I'll be your guide to the captivating shows, lively parades, and exciting events that make your trip to the park truly memorable. Whether you like impressive spectacles, charming performances, or fun celebrations, Disneyland Paris has something unique for you. Get set to dive into a whirlwind of magic and excitement as we delve into the diverse range of entertainment choices waiting for you. Let's jump in and explore the magic together!

Thrilling Shows

Let's start with some heart-pounding excitement at the different shows spread throughout the park. Here are some must-sees:

➢ *The Lion King: Rhythms of the Pride Land*

Enter the magical world of The Lion King and relive memorable moments from this beloved Disney movie. Join Simba, Timon, Pumbaa, and the rest of the pride as they take you on a rhythmic journey filled with music, dance, and heartwarming scenes. Catch this captivating show at the Frontierland Theater, with multiple daily performances to make sure you don't miss out on the magic.

> *Mickey and the Magician*

Get ready to be amazed as Mickey Mouse takes center stage in a magical adventure like no other. Join Mickey as he learns magic from some of Disney's most famous characters, including the Genie, Lumière, and Rafiki. Witness astonishing illusions, captivating storytelling, and unforgettable moments at the Animagique Theater. With several showtimes throughout the day, you'll have plenty of chances to experience the wonder firsthand.

> *Together: A Pixar Musical Adventure*

Go on a musical journey with your favorite Pixar characters in this enchanting live performance. From the fun world of Toy Story to the heartwarming tales of Finding Nemo and more, join Woody, Buzz, Dory, and other beloved characters as they come together for an unforgettable musical extravaganza.

Head to the Studio Theater and let the magic of Pixar fill your heart with joy and laughter.

- *Frozen: A Musical Invitation*

Feel the magic of Arendelle as Elsa, Anna, Kristoff, Sven, and Olaf perform on stage in this enchanting musical adventure. Dive into the world of Frozen and sing along to your favorite songs as the beloved characters bring the story to life before your eyes.

Catch this unforgettable performance at Toon Studio and let the magic of Frozen enchant you.

- *Stitch Live*

Join everyone's favorite mischievous alien, Stitch, for an interactive and entertaining experience like no other. Laugh, sing, and chat with Stitch as he brings his unique fun to the stage. Head to the Production Courtyard and get ready for an unforgettable encounter with this lovable Disney character.

- *Symphony of Colors*

Immerse yourself in a vibrant daytime show featuring a variety of beloved Disney and Pixar characters. From Mickey Mouse and Timon to Joy and Mirabel, experience the magic of Disney as iconic songs and stories come to life before your eyes. Don't miss this colorful celebration near Sleeping Beauty Castle, available until September 30, 2024.

➢ *The Disney Junior Dream Factory*

Join Mickey and Minnie as they take you behind the scenes of musical dream-making in this delightful show for the whole family. Discover the magic of Disney Junior as your favorite characters come to life in this enchanting production. Head to the Production Courtyard for a 20-minute musical journey filled with laughter, music, and fun for all ages.

With a variety of thrilling shows to choose from, Disneyland Paris offers something for everyone to enjoy. Whether you love classic Disney tales, Pixar adventures, or enchanting musical performances, you're sure to be swept away by the magic of these captivating shows. So gather your loved ones, grab your tickets, and get ready for a day filled with laughter, excitement, and unforgettable memories at Disneyland Paris!

Captivating Parades

Imagine walking through the streets of Disneyland Paris, and suddenly, the air is filled with excitement. That's the magic of the Disney parade! Picture this: beloved Disney characters smoothly passing by you on elaborately decorated floats, accompanied by playful music that fills the air with happy memories. It's a sight to see, and you won't want to miss it.

But when and where can you see this amazing sight? The Disney parade usually goes through the streets of Disneyland Park every day in the afternoon or early evening. To make sure you don't miss this enchanting event, it's important to plan ahead. I suggest checking the official Disneyland Paris website for the parade route and exact times. This way, you can position yourself well along the route and get the best spots to view. Believe me; it's worth it!

What to Enjoy at the Disneyland Parade

- **Magical Atmosphere:** Disneyland Paris parades take you to a fanciful world filled with enchanting music, bright colors, and beloved characters, creating an unforgettable, magical atmosphere. As you walk along the parade route, you'll feel the excitement in the air, with anticipation building with every beat of the music.
- **Interactive Entertainment:** Join in the fun as you dance, sing, and interact with your favorite Disney characters during the lively parades, creating shared moments of laughter and joy. Whether you're waving to Cinderella or dancing with Buzz Lightyear, the parades

offer a chance for guests of all ages to be part of the magic.

- **Spectacular Visuals:** Experience stunning floats, dazzling costumes, and amazing choreography that bring Disney stories to life in a visually stunning and captivating way, ensuring a treat for the eyes. From elaborate set designs to detailed costumes, every aspect is carefully crafted to immerse you in the world of Disney like never before.

- **Character Encounters:** Get up close and personal with iconic Disney characters as they wave, pose for photos, and spread happiness, making each parade a unique opportunity for memorable interactions. Whether you're a lifelong fan or experiencing the magic for the first time, the parades offer a chance to connect with your favorite characters in a truly unforgettable way.

- **Timeless Family Bonding:** Disneyland Paris parades provide families with a chance to come together, share in the excitement, and create lasting memories, fostering a sense of joy and togetherness in the most magical place on earth. From grandparents to grandchildren, everyone can join in the fun and create memories that will be cherished for years to come.

Parades at Disneyland Paris

- **A Million Splashes of Color:** This vibrant daytime show brings together beloved Disney and Pixar characters for a celebration of life, diversity, and the power of music. With energetic dancers, catchy tunes, and colorful costumes, it's a feast for the senses that will leave you smiling. Be sure to catch this lively parade at Disneyland from February 10th to September 30th, and join in the fun at Central Plaza, in front of the Sleeping Beauty Castle.

- **Disney Stars on Parade:** While not a traditional parade, this immersive meet-and-greet experience allows you to personally greet Disney and Pixar characters as they stroll through Hollywood Boulevard. Whether you're taking photos, getting autographs, or simply enjoying the magic, it's an unforgettable opportunity to connect with your favorite characters throughout the day.

- **Disney Electrical Sky Parade:** Get ready to be amazed by this skyward spectacle, where hundreds of synchronized drones light up the night sky with vibrant colors and iconic shapes. Inspired by the classic Main Street Electrical Parade, this innovative show precedes the nighttime spectacular "Disney Dreams!" at Disneyland. Don't miss your chance to witness this mesmerizing display of technology and imagination, happening daily after sunset above the Sleeping Beauty Castle.

Seasonal Celebrations

When it comes to seasonal celebrations, Disneyland Paris knows how to create magic, especially during Halloween, Christmas, and New Year's Eve. Let me guide you through the exciting festivities of Halloween at Disneyland Paris.

Disneyland Paris Halloween

Halloween is a fantastic time to enjoy the spooky atmosphere and join in the celebrations, and where better to do so than in the enchanting city of Paris? If you're looking for an unforgettable experience, consider planning your visit to Disneyland Paris during the spooky season.

During this time, the park transforms into a beautifully eerie wonderland, with special events, decorations, and plenty of excitement.

When is Halloween Happening in 2024?

From October 1st to November 5th, Disneyland Paris is adorned in its Halloween best, offering guests a variety of enchanting experiences. Imagine the park decorated with pumpkins, skeletons, and ghosts, creating a spooky yet delightful atmosphere.

As you wander through the park, you'll encounter costumed characters wandering around, adding to the festive mood.

What to expect:

One highlight of the Halloween season at Disneyland Paris is Mickey's Magnificent Halloween Celebration. This exciting event includes a special parade, fireworks show, and a range of spooky activities perfect for families and friends looking for a thrilling time.

But the fun doesn't end there. Throughout the Halloween season, guests can enjoy various activities, including meeting Disney's famous villains, fun Halloween-themed rides for kids, and indulging in spooky treats scattered throughout the park. From pumpkin-inspired dishes at different restaurants to photo opportunities in pumpkin patches with costumed characters, there's something to satisfy every Halloween craving.

Halloween Parties:

And let's not forget about Halloween parties! On October 31st, Disneyland Paris hosts special Halloween-themed gatherings that you won't want to miss. With spooky characters, surprises at every turn, and the festivities lasting until the early hours, these parties offer an unforgettable Halloween experience.

Just keep in mind that as night falls, the atmosphere may get a bit darker with Disney villains around, so it's best to avoid bringing young children or sensitive guests.

What To Do During Halloween at Disneyland Paris:

Of course, no trip to Disneyland Paris during Halloween would be complete without indulging in some spooky souvenirs and treats.

From Mickey Mouse ears with spooky designs to Halloween-themed T-shirts commemorating your visit, the park's shops have something for every Halloween fan.

And when it comes to treats, Disneyland Paris offers everything from themed snacks and candies to apple cider stations for the little ones.

Christmas at Disneyland Paris

Are you dreaming of a wonderful Christmas experience? Well, let me take you on a journey through the charming world of Disneyland Paris during the festive season. From the twinkling lights to the heartwarming performances, there's so much to see and do during the Christmas celebrations at this iconic theme park.

As the holiday season approaches, Disneyland Paris transforms into a winter wonderland, captivating visitors with its festive charm. From November 11th to January 7th, the park comes alive with dazzling decorations, special events, and joyful entertainment, making it the perfect destination for a magical Christmas getaway.

What to Expect:

Disneyland Paris pulls out all the stops to create an unforgettable Christmas experience. The park is adorned with festive lights, immersive decorations, and a palpable sense of holiday cheer. Iconic Disney characters take center stage in Mickey's Dazzling Christmas Parade, a spectacular procession featuring over 50 floats and beloved characters like Mickey, Minnie, and Donald Duck.

You won't want to miss the chance to snap a photo with Santa and your favorite Disney pals during the Meet 'n' Greet sessions.

One of the highlights of the Christmas season is the enchanting "Let's Sing Christmas" musical, where beloved Disney characters serenade guests with classic holiday tunes. From Mickey and Minnie to Goofy and Daisy, the whole gang joins in the festive fun, creating unforgettable memories for guests of all ages.

At nightfall, Disneyland Paris lights up with the magical Disney Dreams! of Christmas event. Hosted by none other than Olaf from Frozen, this enchanting spectacle features dazzling projections, fireworks, and scenes from beloved Disney movies celebrating the spirit of Christmas. You'll be transported to a world of wonder as you watch your favorite characters come to life against the backdrop of Sleeping Beauty Castle.

What to Do During Christmas at Disneyland Paris:

Aside from the enchanting shows and parades, there's plenty more to see and do during Christmas at Disneyland Paris. Take a stroll through a Winter Wonderland, where snow-covered streets and festive decorations create a magical atmosphere.

Don't forget to catch the magical lighting of the Christmas Tree, a heartwarming ceremony that takes place each evening.

If you're in the mood for some holiday shopping, Disneyland Paris has you covered with its array of festive merchandise. From ornaments and souvenirs to delicious treats and gifts, you'll find something for everyone on your list.

After a day of excitement, unwind at one of Disneyland Paris' themed hotels, where you can enjoy the festive atmosphere and special holiday offerings. From complimentary champagne to festive decorations, these hotels provide the perfect backdrop for a memorable Christmas getaway.

And of course, no visit to Disneyland Paris would be complete without indulging in some delicious Christmas-themed treats. From gingerbread cookies to festive-themed snacks, there's no shortage of culinary delights to enjoy during the holiday season.

So, why wait? Pack your bags, gather your loved ones, and embark on a magical Christmas adventure at Disneyland Paris. With its festive decorations, enchanting shows, and joyful atmosphere, it's the perfect place to make lasting memories and celebrate the most wonderful time of the year.

New Year's Eve at Disneyland Paris

Ah, New Year's Eve at Disneyland Paris – it's like entering a magical world where wonders abound and dreams come true. Let me explain why celebrating the New Year at this enchanting place is an experience you'll always remember.

As the clock strikes midnight on December 31st, Disneyland Paris turns into a wonderland of lights, laughter, and endless excitement. The parks and resorts burst with a spectacular fireworks display that lights up the night sky with vibrant colors. It's a breathtaking sight that will leave you amazed and fill your heart with happiness.

One of the greatest things about New Year's Eve at Disneyland Paris is that everyone can join in the celebration. No need for separate tickets – just come and join the fun! Both Disneyland Park and Walt Disney Studios Park will be open from 9 AM to 1 AM, so you'll have plenty of time to enjoy the magic of the event.

What to Do During New Year Celebration at Disneyland Paris:

Firstly, get ready to be captivated by an amazing firework display. Say goodbye to the old year and welcome the new one in grand style as the night sky dazzles with bursts of color and sparkle. It's a truly unforgettable experience that will leave you feeling happy and inspired.

But that's not all – New Year's Eve at Disneyland Paris is also an opportunity to meet some of your favorite Disney characters in their festive outfits. From Mickey and Minnie to Bo Peep and Oogie Boogie, all your beloved characters will be around, spreading joy and laughter. Don't forget to take a photo with them – it's a moment you'll cherish forever.

And of course, what's a visit to Disneyland Paris without enjoying the fantastic rides and attractions? On New Year's Eve, almost all the rides will be open until 1 AM, giving you the chance to experience the magic of Disneyland at night. From thrilling roller coasters to enchanting dark rides, there's something for everyone to enjoy.

What to Expect:

But perhaps the most exciting part is the atmosphere itself. There's a feeling of excitement and anticipation in the air, as people from different backgrounds come together to celebrate the beginning of a new year. Whether you're dancing to the music, watching an incredible show, or simply soaking in the sights and sounds around you, you'll feel a sense of wonder and happiness.

And then, there are the fireworks – the highlight of the evening. As the clock strikes midnight, the sky above Sleeping Beauty Castle bursts into a spectacular display of light and sound, creating a magical ambiance throughout the park. It's a moment of pure enchantment, reminding us of the beauty and magic of Disneyland Paris.

So, if you're searching for a truly memorable way to welcome the New Year, why not join the festivities at Disneyland Paris? It's a celebration like no other, filled with magic, laughter, and memories that will stay with you forever. Come and experience the magic for yourself.

SKIP THE LINE, NIGHT TOURS, AND ENTRANCES

Let's discuss one of the top strategies to maximize your time at Disneyland Paris: avoiding queues, taking night tours, and discovering the optimal entrances. When you're in such a magical setting, you'd rather enjoy the fun than waste time in lengthy lines, correct? That's where these tactics become useful. So, get ready as I guide you through speeding through the parks, exploring after sunset, and diving straight into the thrill!

Skip The Line

Are you ready to jump into the magic of Disneyland Paris without dealing with long lines? As a keen traveler and Disneyland fan, I understand how important it is to skip the lines to get the most out of your visit.

Let me explain why it's crucial to skip the lines and offer some tips to help you reduce wait times and enjoy your time at the parks to the fullest.

Why It's Important to Skip the Line

- **Avoid Crowds:** Disneyland Paris is the biggest theme park in Europe, attracting countless visitors eager to explore its enchanting wonders. But with popularity comes crowds, and maneuvering through masses of people can take away from the magic of your visit. Learning to skip the lines means you can breeze through the attractions easily, avoiding the crush of people.

- **Escape Long Waits:** Some of Disneyland Paris's attractions are famous worldwide, drawing crowds that result in wait times of up to 45 minutes to an hour. Imagine standing in line for that long just for a few minutes of excitement! Knowing how to skip the lines lets you bypass these long queues, so you can spend more time enjoying the attractions instead of waiting in line.

- **Explore the Parks:** With over 50 rides and attractions spread across two captivating theme parks, Disneyland Paris offers a wealth of experiences waiting to be discovered. But time is limited, and trying to do everything in one visit can be tough. By mastering the art of skipping the lines, you'll have

more time to explore the parks and immerse yourself in their magical offerings.
- **Meet Characters:** Meeting beloved Disney characters is a highlight for many visitors, but long lines at attractions can eat into this precious time. By skipping the lines, you'll have more quality moments interacting with your favorite characters, creating unforgettable memories.

Strategies For Reducing Wait Times And Maximizing Park Enjoyment

- **Book Tickets Online:** Save time and skip ticket queues by buying your tickets online beforehand. This not only speeds up your entry process but also lets you take advantage of any exclusive online offers or discounts.
- **Stay at Disneyland Paris Hotels:** Staying at one of Disneyland Paris's onsite hotels not only gives you easy access to the parks but also offers perks like early park entry and extended park hours, so you can beat the crowds and make the most of your visit.

- **Arrive Early:** Get to the parks early to enjoy shorter wait times and fewer crowds. Many visitors tend to arrive later in the day, so starting your day bright and early gives you a head start on experiencing the attractions with minimal wait times.
- **Stay Late:** Alternatively, staying late until the parks close can also be beneficial. As the day goes on, crowds usually thin out, giving you the chance to enjoy popular attractions with shorter wait times.
- **Use Disney Premier Access:** Disneyland Paris offers a convenient paid service called Disney Premier Access, which lets you skip regular lines and enjoy faster access to select attractions. Though it comes with an extra cost, it can be worth it for those who want to make the most of their park experience.
- **Try Single Rider:** For solo travelers or those willing to split up temporarily from their group, using the Single Rider queues can significantly cut down wait times for certain attractions. While you may not ride together with your companions, you'll get faster access and spend less time waiting in line.

Night Tours

When the sun sets and the stars sparkle above, Disneyland Paris changes into a completely different world of magic and wonder. Believe me, seeing Disneyland Paris at night is something you absolutely must do if you're visiting this enchanting place. Let me guide you through the fascinating night tours that will make your Disneyland Paris adventure truly unforgettable.

Why It's Important to Experience Disneyland Paris at Night

Firstly, let me explain why it's essential to visit Disneyland Paris after dark. Imagine this: the Sleeping Beauty Castle lit up by a stunning drone light show. It's like something from a fairy tale, and trust me, witnessing it in person will leave you amazed. The drone lights bring the castle to life in a way you've never seen before, creating memories that will stay with you forever.

And that's just the start! Go to Big Thunder Mountain and get ready to be amazed by the incredible fireworks display. The lighting team at Big Thunder Mountain deserves praise for putting on such an impressive show. Once you've seen the fireworks, you'll want to come back for more, night after night.

But wait, there's more! The rides and attractions at Disneyland Paris become even more exciting at night. For example, take Indiana Jones and the Temple of Peril.

The fire and torches along the ride make it feel even more thrilling after dark. And let's not forget about Le Carrousel de Lancelot and Adventure Isle – they become even more enchanting under the moonlight. And for those who like a good scare, Phantom Manor becomes even spookier once the sun sets.

Information On Nighttime Experiences

Now, let me tell you about some of the nighttime experiences you absolutely have to try at Disneyland Paris.

Firstly, we have Disney Illuminations – the highlight of nighttime entertainment at the park. This amazing show lights up the night sky with fireworks and features Disney's most beloved characters projected onto the Sleeping Beauty Castle. It's a truly magical experience that will leave you feeling warm, fuzzy, and utterly amazed. Make sure to see it at 9:30 PM for a show you'll never forget.

And just before Disney Illuminations begins, don't miss out on Disney D-Light – a fantastic display celebrating Disneyland Paris' 30th Anniversary. With water jets, lighting effects, lasers, and 150 synchronized drones, it's a spectacle unlike any other. Catch it at 9:30 PM for seven minutes of pure Disney magic.

Of course, no nighttime visit to Disneyland Paris would be complete without a comfortable stay at one of the park's hotels and resorts. Consider booking a room at Disney Hotel New York – The Art of Marvel, which boasts the world's largest collection of Marvel artwork. It's the perfect place to relax after a day of excitement.

And finally, take a leisurely walk through the illuminated streets of Disneyland Park. Whether you're there during Christmas or any other time of year, you'll be treated to stunning decorations and themed events. Look out for Disney Dreams! of Christmas, hosted by everyone's favorite snowman, Olaf. It's a heartwarming experience that will fill you with holiday cheer.

Guidance On Park Entrances

When it comes to getting into Disneyland Paris, you have a few easy options. Whether you're taking the metro, bus, or driving, getting to the entrances is simple. The RER train runs to

Disneyland Paris every 15 minutes, dropping you off at the Chessey Station. Also, there are shuttle bus services to the airport and Disneyland Paris Express buses from Paris that you can use.

Once you arrive, you'll find the main entrance of Disneyland Paris accessible via Av. Paul Séramy. Inside, Disneyland Paris is divided into two main areas: Disney Village and Disney Hotels.

1. Disneyland Park Entrance

When you walk through the main gates, you'll see the Disneyland Park entrance on your right. This is the entrance to both Disney Hotels and the first theme park. Disney Village and several Disney Hotels are on your right as you enter. Directly ahead is the Chessey Station, and on your left, you'll find the iconic Disneyland Hotel.

How to get there: The theme park is just behind the Disneyland Hotel. Main Street U.S.A. is the official entrance into the park, leading you to the Sleeping Beauty Castle, the heart of Disneyland Park. While exploring this theme park, expect to walk mostly, although the Disneyland Railroad conveniently connects all four sections of Disneyland Park.

2. Walt Disney Studios Entrance

As you continue through the main gates of Disneyland Paris, you'll come across the entrance to Walt Disney Studios on your left. This park, which opened in 2002, is Disneyland Park's sister park and currently the smallest Disney park worldwide.

The Studio entrance leads you to the Front Lot and is split into four zones based on Disney-Pixar themes. Although it's smaller compared to other Disney parks, Walt Disney Studios still offers memorable experiences at Disneyland Paris.

Choosing the Right Entrance:

- **Disney Hotels:** If you're staying at any of the Disney Hotels, use the Disneyland Park entrance. Once inside, the Disneyland Hotel will be on your left, and other hotels will be on your right.
- **Disney Village:** You can access Disney Village through the Disneyland Park entrance as well, located a short distance ahead of the main entrance and to the right.
- **Theme Parks:** Depending on your theme park tickets, use either the Walt Disney Studios entrance or the Disneyland Park entrance.

RESTAURANTS AND FAMILY TRAVEL

When it comes to eating out and traveling with your family at Disneyland Paris, there are plenty of tasty experiences waiting for you. From fun character meals to fancy food, there's something to please everyone. Come along as we discover the top restaurants and family-friendly places to eat, along with tricks for getting the most out of your food adventures in the enchanting world of Disneyland Paris.

Dining Options Within The Parks And Resort Hotels

Dining at Disneyland Paris is an experience like no other. From the delightful ambiance to the scrumptious food options, every meal promises to be a memorable affair. Let me take you through the enchanting dining options within the parks and resort hotels.

HIGHLIGHTS

- **Dine with Characters:** One of the highlights of dining at Disneyland Paris is the opportunity to share your meal with beloved Disney characters. Imagine Mickey Mouse or Cinderella making a surprise visit to your table! At select restaurants within the park, you can enjoy character dining experiences, where you can interact with your favorite Disney icons, take memorable photos, and even get autographs. It's a magical experience that adds an extra layer of joy to your mealtime.

- **Vegetarian and Vegan Options:** Disneyland Paris caters to all dietary preferences, ensuring that everyone can enjoy a satisfying meal. Whether you're vegetarian, vegan, kosher, or halal, you'll find diverse options to suit your taste buds. Each restaurant offers at least one vegetarian and vegan dish, allowing you to indulge in flavorful creations while adhering to your dietary choices.

- **Themed Dining:** Step into a world of imagination and wonder with themed dining experiences at Disneyland Paris. From cozy American diners to exotic African retreats, each restaurant transports you to a different era or locale. Whether you fancy dining in a colonial-style British retreat or within the lively ambiance of an Old

San Francisco cable car, there's a themed restaurant to suit every preference.

- **Dining Options:** Disneyland Paris offers a variety of dining options to suit every craving and schedule. Whether you're looking for a quick bite on the go, a casual meal at a snack bar, or a leisurely dining experience at a full-fledged table service restaurant, you'll find plenty of choices to satisfy your hunger. Plus, with convenient locations throughout the parks and resort hotels, you're never far from delicious dining options.
- **Lakeside Dining:** For a picturesque dining experience, head to Disney Village overlooking Lake Disney. Here, you can enjoy a late-night meal against the backdrop of shimmering waters and twinkling lights. What's more, some restaurants in the Village are accessible even without a park ticket, making them the perfect spot for a relaxing evening meal or post-park snack.

Disneyland Paris Themed Restaurants

Now, let's explore some of the enchanting themed restaurants that await you at Disneyland Paris:

- **Pizzeria Bella Notte:** Step into the charming world of Lady and the Tramp at this Italian-themed pizzeria. Indulge in mouthwatering pizzas and pasta dishes while surrounded by whimsical decor inspired by the beloved animated film.
- **Cable Car Bake Shop:** Transport yourself to the bustling streets of Old San Francisco at this quaint bake shop. From freshly baked pastries to aromatic coffee blends, this charming eatery offers a delightful taste of vintage California charm.
- **Captain Jack's:** Embark on a culinary adventure with a visit to this pirate-themed restaurant. Set sail with hearty seafood dishes and Caribbean-inspired flavors as you immerse yourself in the swashbuckling atmosphere of Captain Jack's hideaway.
- **Restaurant Hakuna Matata:** Experience the circle of life at this vibrant eatery inspired by The Lion King. Feast on savory African-inspired cuisine while surrounded by colorful murals and playful decor straight out of the Pride Lands.
- **Inventions:** Celebrate the spirit of innovation at this eclectic dining destination. From gourmet delights to inventive culinary creations, Inventions offers a culinary

journey that delights the senses and sparks the imagination.

- **Annette's Diner:** Step back in time to the golden age of rock 'n' roll at this retro diner. With classic American fare and a nostalgic ambiance, Annette's Diner is the perfect spot to indulge in comfort food favorites while enjoying a trip down memory lane.
- **Bistro Chez Remy:** Enter the charming world of "Ratatouille" at this whimsical bistro inspired by the beloved animated film. Dine on French-inspired cuisine in a cozy setting reminiscent of Gusteau's famous restaurant, where even the smallest guest is treated like a culinary connoisseur.

Dining with Disney Characters

One of the most delightful experiences at Disneyland Paris is dining with Disney characters. Imagine enjoying a tasty meal while Mickey Mouse, Cinderella, or other beloved characters come to your table for a meet and greet! It's a dream come true for kids and adults alike. Here are a few restaurants where you can enjoy this magical experience:

- **Cinderella Inn:** Step into the fairy tale world of Cinderella and her friends at this charming restaurant, where you can dine in a medieval setting and meet Disney princesses.
- **Plaza Gardens Restaurant:** Located on Main Street, USA, this classy restaurant offers a buffet-style dining experience with visits from classic Disney characters.
- **Inventions:** Situated in the Disneyland Hotel, Inventions is known for its extravagant brunches and dinners featuring a wide array of Disney characters.
- **Cafe Mickey:** Located in Disney Village, Cafe Mickey offers a lively atmosphere and delicious meals, with visits from Mickey and his pals to enhance your dining experience.

Meal Plan at Disneyland Paris:

To make your Disney vacation even more enjoyable, you can opt for a Disney Dining Plan, which allows you to pre-pay for your meals and enjoy a stress-free dining experience. There are three meal plan options available: Standard, Plus, and Extra Plus.

- **Standard:** With this plan, you can choose from a variety of restaurants and enjoy sit-down meals, on-the-go meals, or all-you-can-eat buffets. Prices start at EUR 28.86 per night.

- **Plus:** This plan offers access to a wide range of dining options, including sit-down meals, on-the-go meals, and buffets. Prices start at EUR 35.82 per night.
- **Extra Plus:** The most luxurious option, this plan includes full-board dining, a character dining experience, and additional beverages. Prices start at EUR 67.15 per night.

Types of Disneyland Paris Restaurants

When it comes to eating options within the parks and resort hotels at Disneyland Paris, there's something to suit every preference and hunger. Let me guide you on a food journey through the different kinds of restaurants and places to eat you can find spread throughout the enchanting world of Disneyland Paris.

1. *On-The-Go:*
    - If you're on-the-go and need a quick snack to keep your energy up for all the adventures awaiting you, there are several spots you'll want to check out:
    - **Cookie Kitchen:** Located in Disneyland Park on Main Street USA, Cookie Kitchen is the perfect place to indulge your sweet tooth. From delicious pastries to

mouthwatering cookies, you'll find an array of treats to satisfy your cravings. And if you need a quick drink to go along with your snack, they've got you covered. With prices averaging around EUR 20 for two, it's a tasty and budget-friendly option.

- **Cool Post:** Nestled in Adventureland, Cool Post offers refreshing snacks and drinks to help you recharge before diving back into your Disney adventure. Whether you need a cold drink or a quick snack, this African-styled outpost has just what you need to keep the fun going.

- **Cool Stop:** For a taste of American classics, swing by Cool Stop in Disney Village. From pancakes to hot dogs to sweet snacks, this drive-through eatery has something for everyone. It's the perfect place for a quick and satisfying meal.

- **Bush Cafe:** Another gem in Adventureland, Bush Cafe immerses you in African-inspired surroundings as you enjoy refreshing drinks and snacks. With its unique atmosphere and delicious offerings, it's a must-visit during your Disneyland Paris journey.

- **Cool Station:** Calling all Star Wars fans! Cool Station in Discoveryland is your go-to spot for themed drinks and snacks straight out of the beloved universe. Whether you're craving a lightsaber-shaped treat or a refreshing drink, this futuristic station has you covered.

- **Ice Cream Creations:** Treat yourself to a deliciously cool break at Ice Cream Creations in Production Courtyard. Inspired by Disney Classics, these ice creams are made right before your eyes, ensuring a fresh and flavorful experience.
- **Fan-tastic Food Truck:** Make a pit stop at this food truck in Marvel Avengers Campus for a taste of New York classics. From hot dogs to sweet treats, it's a fantastic spot to refuel before continuing your superhero adventures.
- **Laugh'N' Go:** Take a Pixar-themed break at Laugh'N' Go in Worlds of Pixar. With hot and cold drinks, as well as exclusive sweet and savory snacks, it's the perfect place to relax and recharge.
- **The Enchanted Tree:** Escape the heat at The Enchanted Tree in Fantasyland. This cozy hut under a magical tree offers seasonal snacks and fruity drinks to help you beat the heat and keep your energy up for more Disney fun.
- **WEB Food Truck:** For a taste of Asia, head to the WEB Food Truck in Marvel Avengers Campus. Watch as your noodle dish with chicken, prawn, or smoked tofu

is prepared right before your eyes, transporting your taste buds to a whole new world of flavor.

- **The Old Mill:** Drawing inspiration from Walt Disney's timeless short film, The Old Mill, this charming haven nestled in Fantasyland provides an array of beverages, ice creams, and popcorn flavors to delight your taste buds.
- **Toon Studio Catering Co.:** Finally, in Toon Studio, you'll find Toon Studio Catering Co., where you can order a crepe or ice cream paired with a hot or cold drink for the perfect snack break.

2. *All-you-can-eat Buffets:*
- **Chuck Wagon Café:** Step into the cozy atmosphere of Chuck Wagon Café at Disney Hotel Cheyenne for a hearty meal. Enjoy tasty salads, barbeque ribs, and sip on refreshing beverages. Open for dinner from 6 PM to 10:30 PM, this Tex-Mex haven offers a taste of the Wild West with a price range of EUR 76 for two.
- **Cape Cod:** Located at Disney Newport Bay Club, Cape Cod specializes in seafood dishes in a Mediterranean-inspired setting. From fish to salads and desserts, there's

something for everyone. With a price range of EUR 80 for two, immerse yourself in the flavors of the sea.

- **Downtown Restaurant:** Explore a variety of cuisines at Downtown Restaurant in Disney Hotel New York. From American to Italian and Chinese dishes, this buffet caters to diverse tastes. Open from 6 PM to 11 PM, indulge in a multi-cuisine experience for EUR 84 for two.

- **The Cellar:** Embark on a culinary journey along Route 66 at The Cellar in Disney Hotel Santa Fe. Delight in Tex-Mex specialties in a vibrant market-themed setting. With a price range of EUR 42 for two, savor the flavors of the Southwest from 6 PM to 10:30 PM.

- **PYM Kitchen:** Dive into the world of experimental cuisine at PYM Kitchen in Marvel Avengers Campus. From large burgers to small croutons, this lab-inspired restaurant offers a unique dining experience. Explore their diverse menu with a price range of EUR 84 for two.

- **Restaurant Agrabah Cafe:** Transport yourself to the heart of Agrabah at Adventureland and indulge in Middle Eastern cuisine at Restaurant Agrabah Cafe. With a price range of EUR 76 for two, savor the exotic flavors amidst Aladdin-themed surroundings.

- **Plaza Gardens Restaurant:** Experience Victorian elegance at Plaza Gardens Restaurant in Disneyland Park - Main Street USA. Known for its character dining, this restaurant offers a French-inspired menu with a price range of EUR 82 for two.

3. *Table Service:*
    - **Annette's Diner:** Step back in time at Annette's Diner in Disney Village and enjoy classic American favorites. From hamburgers to hot dogs and milkshakes, this diner offers a nostalgic dining experience for EUR 40 for two.
    - **Brasserie Rosalie:** Indulge in French cuisine with a view at Brasserie Rosalie in Disney Village. With a picturesque setting overlooking Disney Lake, this brasserie offers a taste of France amidst elegant surroundings.
    - **Silver Spur Steakhouse:** Treat yourself to perfectly grilled steaks at Silver Spur Steakhouse in Frontierland. With meal plans available, enjoy an exquisite dining experience for EUR 80 for two.
    - **Manhattan Restaurant:** Delight in Italian flavors at Manhattan Restaurant in Disney Hotel New York. From

creamy risotto to antipasto, this restaurant offers a taste of Italy for EUR 60 for two.

- **Captain Jack's - Pirate Restaurant:** Embark on a culinary adventure at Captain Jack's in Adventureland. With a torch-lit pirate ambiance and a treasure trove of Caribbean-inspired dishes, this restaurant offers an unforgettable dining experience for EUR 84 for two.
- **The Lucky Nugget Saloon:** Step into the Wild West at The Lucky Nugget Saloon in Frontierland. From burgers to steaks, this cowboy hangout spot offers classic American fare for EUR 44 for two.

4. *Bars:*

- **Red Garter Saloon:** Immerse yourself in cowboy culture at Red Garter Saloon in Disney Hotel Cheyenne. Enjoy a cold beer and share tales from the frontier in this old-country joint.
- **Bleeker Street Lounge:** Unwind at Bleeker Street Lounge in Disney Hotel New York - The Art of Marvel. From craft beers to mocktails, this loft-styled bar offers a relaxing retreat with a view of the lake.
- Crockett's Saloon: Quench your thirst at Crockett's Saloon in Disney Davy Crockett Ranch. With rustic

charm and a game of pool, this pioneer's saloon is the perfect spot to unwind.

- **Billy Bob's Country Western Saloon:** Experience the lively atmosphere of Billy Bob's in Disney Village. From cocktails to coffee, this saloon offers a vibrant nightlife scene with a dance floor open on weekends.
- **Redwood Bar and Lounge:** Cozy up by the fireplace at Redwood Bar and Lounge in Disney Sequoia Lodge. Sip on a cocktail and relax in this wooden lodge-inspired setting.

5. *Quick-service Restaurants:*
- **New York Style Sandwiches:** If you're in the mood for a quick bite with an American touch, head over to the fast-paced deli in Disney Village. Here, you can enjoy various choices from the salad bar, hot or cold deli sandwiches, pasta, and hotdogs. The deli offers indoor seating for your convenience, making it a perfect stop during your Disneyland Paris adventure. Expect to spend around EUR 30 for two.
- **Cafe Hyperion:** Step into the future at Cafe Hyperion in Discoveryland, where you can watch movies or shows while enjoying classic fast-food favorites like burgers

and nuggets. Don't forget to check out the Star Wars collectibles while you're there! A meal for two will cost around EUR 40.

- **Cowboy Cookout Barbecue:** Transport yourself to the Wild West at Cowboy Cookout Barbecue in Frontierland. Indulge in mouthwatering barbecue delights accompanied by lively tunes. Expect to spend around EUR 34 for two.

- **Last Chance Cafe:** For a taste of Tex-Mex cuisine, look no further than Last Chance Cafe in Frontierland. Whether you're looking for a quick bite or a hearty meal, this Old West outpost has got you covered.

- **Colonel Hathi's Pizza Outpost:** Craving Italian cuisine? Head to Colonel Hathi's Pizza Outpost in Disneyland Park for Mickey Mouse-shaped pizzas, pasta, and more. With a colonial-style British ambiance, this eatery offers a unique dining experience.

- **Hep Cat Corner:** Follow the jazz tunes to Hep Cat Corner in Walt Disney Studios Park, where you can enjoy muffins, doughnuts, refreshing drinks, and ice creams.

- **At the Marionette Chalet:** Experience German delights at Au Chalet de la Marionnette in Fantasyland, inspired by the world of Pinocchio.

- **Toad Hall Restaurant:** For classic English fish and chips, head to Toad Hall Restaurant in Fantasyland. This countryside British eatery is perfect for a satisfying meal.
- **Restaurant Hakuna Matata:** Embark on a culinary journey to Africa at Restaurant Hakuna Matata in Adventureland. Feast on delicious African quick bites in this Lion King-themed eatery.
- **Market House Deli:** In Main Street U.S.A., Market House Deli offers a taste of early 20th-century New York with its selection of hot and cold skyscraper sandwiches and subs.

6. *Snack Bars:*

- **McDonald's:** For familiar comfort food, McDonald's in Disney Village offers burgers, fries, cokes, and ice creams.
- **Rainforest Café:** Experience dining among the Amazonians at Rainforest Café in Disney Village, complete with rainforest sounds and ambiance.
- **Starbucks Coffee:** Indulge in freshly brewed coffee and a variety of teas and snacks at Starbucks Coffee in Disney Village.

- **Earl of Sandwich:** Overlooking Lake Disney in Disney Village, Earl of Sandwich serves up warm meat, cheese, and vegetarian subs without requiring park tickets.
- **King Ludwig's Castle:** Step into a royal banquet hall at King Ludwig's Castle in Disney Village and enjoy German burgers, sausages, and chocolate desserts, along with famous beers on tap.
- **Vapiano:** Experience the flavors of Italy at Vapiano in Disney Village, where every dish is made from fresh ingredients.

With such a wide array of dining options, Disneyland Paris ensures that every visitor's taste buds are treated to a magical culinary experience. So, whether you're craving American classics, Tex-Mex delights, or European flavors, there's something for everyone to enjoy during your visit.

Recommendations For Family-Friendly Dining Experiences

When it comes to eating at Disneyland Paris with your family, you want to make sure that everyone, from the little ones to the adults, enjoys tasty meals while making memorable moments together. Let me share some suggestions for family-friendly dining experiences that will please every taste and make your visit even more special.

Character Dining Experiences: One of the most magical ways to dine at Disneyland Paris is by enjoying a character dining experience. These meals not only offer delicious food but also give your family a chance to meet beloved Disney characters up close. From having breakfast with Mickey Mouse to dinner with Disney princesses, there's a character dining option to suit everyone's preferences. Make sure to book ahead to secure your spot and create unforgettable memories with your favorite characters.

Buffet Restaurants: Buffet-style dining is great for families with choosy eaters or those who like a variety of options. Disneyland Paris has several buffet restaurants where you can enjoy a range of dishes, from different cuisines to familiar comfort foods. The buffet setup lets everyone pick their favorites and enjoy as much as they want, making it a perfect choice for families with varying tastes and appetites.

Quick-Service Restaurants: When you're busy exploring the parks and don't want to spend too much time on a sit-down meal, quick-service restaurants are the way to go.

These places offer convenient and tasty options that are perfect for families on the move. From burgers and sandwiches to salads and snacks, you'll find plenty of quick and satisfying meals to keep you going on your adventures. Plus, many quick-service restaurants have meals tailored for kids, making them popular with the little ones.

Themed Dining Experiences: Immerse yourself in Disney magic by dining at themed restaurants that bring your favorite stories to life. Whether you're dining in a pirate ship at Captain Jack's - Restaurant des Pirates or enjoying Italian food at Bella Notte, themed dining experiences add an extra dash of excitement to your meal. Your family will enjoy the immersive atmosphere and themed decorations while relishing delicious food inspired by Disney movies and characters.

Snack Stops and Treats: Don't forget to treat yourself to some sweet and savory snacks during your day at Disneyland Paris. From churros and popcorn to ice cream and crepes, there are plenty of snack choices to satisfy your cravings between meals. Make sure to try some iconic Disney snacks like Mickey-shaped treats and themed desserts for an extra sprinkle of magic.

Allergy-Friendly Options: If you or someone in your family has dietary restrictions or food allergies, don't worry— Disneyland Paris offers various allergy-friendly dining options.

Many restaurants can cater to special dietary needs, including gluten-free, dairy-free, and vegetarian/vegan options. Just let the staff know about your dietary requirements, and they will do their best to accommodate your needs.

The Right Place To Go Shopping

When you're at Disneyland Paris, shopping becomes more than just a task – it turns into an adventure filled with magic and surprises. With 63 shops spread across the Disneyland Park, Walt Disney Studios, Disney Village, and the official Disney Hotels, there's a treasure trove of delights waiting to be discovered.

One of the most exciting parts of shopping at Disneyland Paris is the wide variety of stores and products available. From trendy t-shirts to unique jewelry, from toys to electronics, there's something to fit every taste and interest. And what makes it even more special is the Disneyland Paris Collection, offering exclusive merchandise that lets you bring a piece of the magic home with you.

Let me guide you through some of the enchanting shops you'll find at Disneyland Park, each with its own unique charm and offerings.

Stores Nestled Within Disneyland Park Paris

1. Main Street

Emporium: This grand store boasts Victorian-style decor and houses the largest selection of souvenirs. Here, you'll find everything from artwork to costumes to toys, making it a must-visit spot for any Disneyland shopper.

Harrington's Fine China & Porcelains: Explore the world of art and collectibles with stunning pieces featuring beloved Disney characters.

Disney & Co.: Step back in time at this vintage toy store and discover your favorite Disney characters and outfits.

Dapper Dan's Hair Cuts: Need a haircut? Head to this vintage barber shop for a trim that will have you looking stylish for your Disneyland adventures.

The Storybook Store: Immerse yourself in the world of Disney stories with a selection of books, movies, and stationary featuring iconic characters.

Disney Clothiers: Show off your Disney style with clothes and accessories inspired by your favorite characters.

Plaza East Boutique and Lilly's Boutique: From precious collectibles to cozy souvenirs, these boutiques offer a variety of gifts and household items to suit any taste.

2. Discoveryland

Star Traders: Embark on a space adventure with clothes, accessories, and toys inspired by the Star Wars universe.

Starport Photographs: Capture memories with a photo alongside Darth Vader, available in print or digital format.

Constellations: Dive into the worlds of Toy Story and Marvel with a selection of space-themed plush toys, souvenirs, and gifts.

3. Adventureland

Temple Traders Boutique: Gear up for adventure with travel-themed products and accessories.

The Captain's Chest: Embrace your inner pirate with clothes, accessories, and souvenirs inspired by Pirates of the Caribbean.

Indiana Jones Adventure Outpost: Take a break from your adventures and explore a selection of themed merchandise.

4. Fantasyland

The Three Fairies Confectionery: Treat yourself with chocolates and sweets fit for royalty.

The Castle Boutique: Experience the magic of Christmas year-round with festive goodies.

Meet Mickey Mouse Photographs: Capture memories with everyone's favorite mouse at his clubhouse.

Sir Mickey's Boutique: Explore medieval-themed merchandise and costumes inspired by beloved Disney stories.

Merlin l'Enchanteur: Discover treasures in this sorcerer's cave, featuring jewelry and artisan glassware.

5. Frontierland

Thunder Mesa Mercantile Building: Get into the spirit of the Wild West with clothes, toys, and treats inspired by frontier life.

Stores Nestled Within Walt Disney Studios Park Paris

1. Worlds of Pixar

Toy Story Playland Boutique: If you love Toy Story as much as I do, you'll be thrilled with the variety of realistic toys and merchandise featuring your favorite characters. From action figures to soft toys, this store has everything you could want.

Chez Marianne (Paris Souvenirs): Step into this beautifully decorated hub filled with delicious sweets and items from the movie Ratatouille. You can find clothing, accessories, and unique gifts here.

2. Production Courtyard

Tower Hotel Gifts: After enjoying the excitement of the Twilight Zone Tower of Terror, why not capture the memory with a photo or shop for trendy clothes and classic Disney items? This store has a wide range of products for everyone.

3. Hollywood Legends: Attention Marvel and Star Wars fans! This shop is just for you, with everything from clothing and accessories to toys and special items.

Don't miss the chance to make your own lightsaber and feel like you're in another galaxy.

4. Front Lot

Walt Disney Studios Store: Situated at the entrance to Walt Disney Studio Park, this shop honors Walt Disney's vision. With a large selection of items, including clothing, accessories, and souvenirs, it's the perfect place to find that special Disney keepsake.

Hollywood Legends: Marvel and Star Wars fans will feel right at home in this store, which offers a variety of products, from clothing and accessories to toys and collectibles. Don't forget to check out the customizable lightsabers!

Stores Nestled Within Disney Village Paris

World of Disney: This shop, inspired by travel, is a must-visit for Disney fans. From costumes to collectibles, you'll find everything you need to bring a touch of Disney magic home.

Boutique Planet Hollywood: Offering a unique shopping experience combined with a restaurant, this store lets you browse clothing, accessories, and more while enjoying the atmosphere of Planet Hollywood.

The LEGO Store: Immerse yourself in the world of Disney with LEGO sets and let your creativity soar. Whether you're building your favorite scenes or creating new adventures, this store has something for every LEGO fan.

Stores Nestled Within Disneyland Hotels Paris

General Store: Located at Disney's Hotel Cheyenne, this western-themed shop offers a wide range of collectibles, souvenirs, and treats. It's the perfect place to pick up a reminder of your Disneyland Paris adventure.

La Vallée Village Chic Outlet Shopping: Found at Disney's Hotel Cheyenne, this outlet shopping destination is perfect for fashion lovers. With top brands and stylish options, it's the ideal spot for a bit of shopping therapy.

Bay Boutique: At Disney's Newport Bay Club, you'll discover a selection of Mickey Mouse collectibles, Pandora-designed Disney products, and more. It's a great place to grab a souvenir or two before you leave.

New York Boutique: Situated at Disney's Hotel New York - The Art of Marvel, this store is a haven for superhero fans. From clothing and accessories to everyday items and collectibles, there's something for every Marvel enthusiast.

Goofy's Pro Shop: Golf lovers won't want to miss this store at Disney's Hotel Cheyenne. Stocked with clothing and accessories, it's the perfect place to get ready for a day on the golf course.

Alamo Trading Post: Transport yourself to the past at Disney's Davy Crockett Ranch and explore this old-style trading post. With gifts and souvenirs for all ages, it's the perfect place to grab a memento of your Disneyland Paris adventure.

Northwest Passage: Finally, immerse yourself in nature at Disney's Sequoia Lodge. This shop offers apparel, accessories, and souvenirs inspired by the great outdoors.

With so many fantastic shopping options available, Disneyland Paris truly is a paradise for shoppers. Whether you're looking for the perfect souvenir or simply enjoying a bit of shopping, you're sure to find something that brings you joy and inspiration.

Tips For Traveling With Children

Traveling with kids can be exciting and tough, but with a bit of planning and some helpful tips, you can make your family trip to Disneyland Paris amazing for everyone. As someone who travels a lot and is a parent myself, I've learned some useful tricks that I'm eager to share with you. So, let's get into some practical advice on getting the most out of your family vacation at the happiest place on earth!

When you're going to Disneyland Paris with kids, it's crucial to plan in advance. Involve the kids in preparing for the trip by talking about what they're looking forward to seeing and doing at the parks. This builds excitement and helps you plan your schedule based on what they want. Also, remember to pack lots of snacks, water bottles, and things to keep them entertained during the journey.

Once you're at Disneyland Paris, pacing yourself is important. There's so much to do that you might want to try and do it all in one day, but that can tire everyone out quickly. Instead, think about spreading your visit over several days and focus on the most important attractions each day. Make sure to include breaks for rest and downtime so the kids can recharge.

Using strollers in the parks can be really helpful when you have kids. They not only give tired little legs a break but also provide a handy place to keep snacks, drinks, and souvenirs. Just make sure to put something distinctive on your stroller to make it easy to find among the others.

Mealtime with hungry kids can be chaotic, so it's smart to plan where you'll eat ahead of time. Disneyland Paris has lots of family-friendly restaurants and quick-service options for every taste and budget. Consider booking your meals in advance to avoid long waits, especially during busy times. And don't forget to bring along some snacks and water to keep hunger at bay between meals.

Meeting Disney characters is a big part of the fun at Disneyland Paris. To make the most of it, try to arrive early for character meet-and-greets to avoid long waits and get more chances for photos. Encourage your kids to talk to the characters by asking questions or sharing their favorite Disney memories. These special moments will be remembered for years to come.

Make sure to take breaks throughout the day to rest, recharge, and make lasting memories with your family. Whether it's enjoying a relaxing boat ride around the park or watching the amazing fireworks show at night, these moments together are what family vacations are all about.

VISITOR TIPS

In this Visitor Tips section, I've gathered all the insider secrets to make your Disneyland Paris adventure unforgettable. Throughout my travels and experiences, I've picked up some valuable tips that I'm thrilled to share with you. From managing crowds to capturing those magical moments, let's ensure you have the best time possible at Disneyland Paris. So, let's dive in and discover how to make the most of your visit!

Insider Tips And Tricks For A Successful Visit

Alright, let me share some insider advice to make sure your trip to Disneyland Paris is a big success. Based on my own experiences and insights, these simple yet effective strategies can make your time in the magical world of Disney even better.

- First, booking tickets to attractions ahead of time is a game-changer. Trust me, you don't want to waste time standing in long lines when you could be enjoying Disneyland Paris. By getting your tickets early, you'll breeze through the gates and dive straight into the fun.

- Another smart move is to buy Shuttle or Express Train tickets. Getting to Disneyland Paris should be exciting, not a hassle. Choosing convenient transportation like shuttles or express trains can save you time and stress, leaving you with more energy to explore.
- Now, let's talk about timing. If you can, try to visit on a weekday. Weekends are busier, with more people and longer waits for rides. By picking a weekday, you'll have shorter lines and a more relaxed vibe, making your Disney experience smoother.
- Comfort is important when you're in the parks, so remember to wear comfy shoes. You'll be doing a lot of walking, and you don't want sore feet ruining your fun. Wear supportive shoes to keep comfortable from morning to night.
- All that excitement is sure to make you hungry, so bring water and snacks. Staying hydrated and fueled up will keep your energy levels high for all the adventures.
- Think about staying in a Disney hotel for the ultimate experience. You'll be super close to the magic, with perks like early park access and easy transportation.

Plus, the themed decor and Disney hospitality will make your stay unforgettable.
- When it's time for rides, timing matters. Go to the popular ones early in the morning or late at night to avoid crowds. You'll have shorter waits and might even squeeze in a few extra rides.
- Before you go to the parks, decide which rides you want to go on. With so many choices, having a plan will help you make the most of your visit and make sure you don't miss anything.
- And lastly, keep a map with you. While getting lost in Disneyland Paris is part of the fun, having a map will help you find your way around and make sure you don't miss any cool spots.

So there you have it, my insider advice for a great trip to Disneyland Paris. With a bit of planning, you'll make memories that last a lifetime in the happiest place on earth.

Suggestions For Managing Crowds

Let's explore some strategies for managing crowds to enhance your Disneyland Paris experience.

As someone who has been there and maneuvered through busy crowds myself, I've gathered some useful tips along the way.

It's important to plan your visit wisely. Disneyland Paris tends to be busiest during peak times like school holidays and weekends. If you can, consider visiting during quieter times, such as weekdays outside major holidays, to avoid large crowds. Arriving early in the morning can also give you a head start before the crowds arrive.

Once you're in the park, make sure to prioritize the attractions you most want to see. Create a list of your favorites and aim to visit them first thing in the morning when lines are usually shorter. Use the Disneyland Paris app or grab a park map to check ride wait times and plan your route accordingly.

Another useful tip is to make use of FastPasses. These convenient tickets allow you to reserve access to certain attractions, significantly reducing your wait time. Be strategic about when you use your FastPasses, saving them for popular rides with the longest lines.

Now, let's discuss navigating through the crowds. It's inevitable that you'll encounter congestion, especially in busy areas like Main Street or around popular attractions. One trick is to walk along the edges of pathways rather than through the middle of the crowds. This can help you move more quickly and avoid getting stuck in bottlenecks.

If you're with a group, consider using a buddy system to stay together in crowded areas. Choose a meeting spot in case you get separated, and ensure everyone can communicate, whether it's via cell phones or walkie-talkies.

When it's time to eat, try to dine during quieter times to avoid long lines at restaurants and food stands. Consider bringing your own snacks and water bottles to keep you going between meals and stay hydrated throughout the day.

Remember to take breaks when needed. Disneyland Paris can be overwhelming with its sights, sounds, and excitement, so it's important to listen to your body and take a break when you start feeling tired or overwhelmed. Find a quiet spot to sit and recharge, whether it's a shady bench or a less crowded area of the park.

Interesting Facts About Disneyland Paris

Let me share some interesting facts about Disneyland Paris that will add a touch of magic to your visit.

- Surprising Location: Did you know that Disneyland Paris wasn't initially planned for its current spot? Yeah, surprising, right? Disney was actually looking at places with warmer weather like Florida or California. But guess what? Paris became the chosen location because it's just a two-hour flight from Central Europe.

- Heart-Pounding Moment: Imagine this: You're exploring Frontierland's Haunted Manor and stumble upon a huge grave in the cemetery. Get close, and you might hear something spooky—a beating heart! Yep, that's right. It's one of Disneyland Paris' best-kept secrets, and oh boy, it's chilling!

- Colorful Illusions: Have you ever noticed the colors in the theme park playing tricks on you? Take a photo of the palace guards or the raven statue with a flash, and see them change colors! Pink and blue guards, red-eyed ravens—talk about a colorful surprise!

- Unexpected Wildlife: Hold onto your Mickey ears because you might just come across some unexpected guests—wild animals! Yep, Disneyland Paris has its own "Wildlife" department taking care of these furry friends. Imagine spotting a fox relaxing in the Peter Pan ride—wild, right?

- Optical Illusion: Here's something to ponder. Ever felt like Main Street was larger than life? Well, that's because of a little trick called forced perspective. As you stroll down, the buildings seem to stretch, making the castle appear farther away. It's all about that Disney magic!
- Historical Figures: Step into Main Street, and you're stepping into history. Take a close look at the storefronts, and you'll see names like Walt Disney and Martin Sklar. These are the people who brought Disneyland Paris to life, and they're honored right here on Main Street!
- Beautiful Castle: The Sleeping Beauty Castle isn't just a sight to see—it's a masterpiece crafted by stained-glass expert Paul Chapman. With inspiration from Mont Saint-Michel and adorned with 24-karat gold leaves, this castle is pure magic.
- Creative Minds: Ever wondered who's behind the scenes making the magic happen? Names like Jeff Burke and Tom Morris aren't just random—they're the masterminds behind Discoveryland and Fantasyland. Next time you see a poster, remember, these are the visionaries!
- Magical Conversations: Ah, the Market House Deli—a hidden gem on Main Street. Inside, you'll find a vintage

phone booth with a magical secret. Pick up the receiver, and listen in on whimsical conversations that'll make you smile!

- Hidden Mickeys: Keep your eyes peeled for hidden Mickeys scattered throughout the park. From building designs to rust spots on treasure boxes, you never know where these iconic symbols might appear!
- Secret Passageways: Ever wondered how characters move from one end of the park to another without getting stuck in crowds? Well, there are hidden tunnels beneath Disneyland Paris, ensuring the magic stays alive above ground!

CONCLUSION

Recap Of Key Points And Highlights From The Guide

As we finish our trip through Disneyland Paris, let's pause to think about all the amazing moments and important tips we've talked about in this detailed travel guide. It's been quite an exciting journey, hasn't it? So, grab your favorite drink and let's go over everything together!

1. First, we explored the wonderful world of Disneyland Paris with a quick history lesson and looked at its special cultural parts and themes. From the famous Sleeping Beauty Castle to the fantastic rides inspired by beloved Disney movies, Disneyland Paris truly offers a unique experience that's different from other Disney parks around the world.

2. Then, we made sure you were ready for your visit by giving you important information before you go. We talked about the best times to visit, considering things like weather, crowds, and special events. Whether you're planning a quick one-day trip or a relaxed three-day vacation, we've got you

covered with sample schedules designed for different types of travelers.

3. Navigating the parks and facilities might seem overwhelming, but don't worry! We shared helpful tips to help you make the most of your visit, including information for guests with different needs. Plus, we covered everything from what to pack to park rules and guidelines, making sure you're fully prepared for a smooth experience at Disneyland Paris.

4. Planning your visit was made simple with detailed information about opening times, places to stay, and booking advice. Whether you're staying at one of the charming hotels on-site or looking at rentals nearby, we gave you guidance to find the perfect place for your magical adventure.

5. Getting to Disneyland Paris and knowing about the facilities on-site are important parts of your trip. We talked about transportation choices, parking details, and pointed out important facilities like bathrooms, first aid stations, and baby care centers to make sure you're comfortable and well taken care of during your visit.

6. Of course, the heart of Disneyland Paris is its amazing theme parks: Disneyland Park and Walt Disney Studios. We took a close look at attractions, rides, shows, and places to

eat, uncovering must-see spots and hidden treasures along the way. From exciting roller coasters to meeting your favorite characters, there's something for everyone to enjoy!

7. No trip to Disneyland Paris would be complete without experiencing its lively entertainment and special events. We talked about seasonal celebrations like Halloween, Christmas, and New Year's Eve, and gave you insider tips for having the best time during these festive times.

8. For those who want to avoid waiting in lines and make the most of their park time, we offered strategies for reducing wait times and having the most fun. Whether you're interested in special tours, nighttime activities, or just finding the easiest way into the parks, we've got you covered.

9. Hungry for adventure? We explored the delicious food options at Disneyland Paris, looking at restaurants in the parks and hotels. From themed dining spots to places perfect for families, we made a list of recommendations to satisfy every appetite.

10. Traveling with little ones? We shared helpful tips for making family vacations unforgettable, making sure everyone has a great time. From renting strollers to finding attractions for kids, Disneyland Paris is a magical place for families to explore together.

As we finish our journey, I want to thank you for coming along with me on this magical trip through Disneyland Paris. Whether it's your first visit or you're a Disney fan, I hope this guide has given you useful information and inspiration for your own magical adventure. Remember, the magic of Disneyland Paris is waiting for you.

Final Thouths

As your guide through the wonderful world of Disneyland Paris, I've shared with you my tips, insights, and suggestions to make your visit unforgettable. But now, I want to hear from you! Yes, you, with your own stories of excitement and exploration.

Visiting Disneyland Paris is more than just enjoying the rides and shows—it's about making memories that will stay with you forever. And what better way to enrich our journey together than by sharing those moments with each other?

Whether you're a first-time visitor or a seasoned Disney fan, I invite you to join me in this online space to exchange stories, swap tips, and relive the magic of Disneyland Paris.

Maybe you stumbled upon a hidden treasure in the parks—a peaceful spot where you could take a break and enjoy the enchantment. Or perhaps you discovered a delicious snack that became your favorite treat during the day. Whatever it is, I want to hear all about it!

Share your experiences, whether they're big or small, funny or heartwarming. Did you conquer your fears on an exciting ride, or did you dance with your favorite Disney characters in a lively parade? Did you find a cozy spot to watch the fireworks, or did you make new friends while waiting in line for your favorite ride?

No story is too insignificant or too grand. Your adventures bring Disneyland Paris to life, and by sharing them, you're adding to the magic for others who are planning their own trip.

But it's not just about sharing the best parts. If you faced any challenges during your visit, like dealing with crowds, finding a good place to eat, or managing your time well, your insights could help fellow travelers overcome similar hurdles.

Your feedback is incredibly valuable, not just to me but to the entire Disneyland Paris community. Together, we can create a treasure trove of insider advice that will make future visitors' experiences even better.

And remember, the magic of Disneyland Paris doesn't end when you leave the park. Whether you're reminiscing about your last visit or dreaming of your next one, know that you're always welcome here.

Thank you for being a part of this amazing journey. I'm excited to hear all about your Disneyland Paris adventures!

Printed in Great Britain
by Amazon

06458a7e-4f8f-4689-a050-9a7ed1721497R01